The Historical Families of Dumfriesshire and the Border Wars

A History of Scottish Nobility

By C. L. Johnstone

PANTIANOS
CLASSICS

Published by Pantianos Classics

ISBN-13: 978-1-78987-065-7

First published in 1878

Contents

Preface

In a previous edition, I alluded too briefly to the important Border war of the reigns of Robert Bruce and Edward I., but as the three claimants to the Scottish throne possessed lands in Dumfriesshire, who naturally took much share in it, I have added a Chapter on the subject. In describing the different families celebrated in past ages, I have given greater prominence to those whose history has never been published before, and who are still represented in the legitimate male line. Owing to the custom of the sons of heiresses inheriting their mother's name, and of lands being rarely entailed exclusively on male heirs, it is a very unusual circumstance to find two branches of one family claiming unbroken male descent from the 15th century, as is the case with the Johnstones, who numbered nine lairds (more than any other house in Dumfriesshire) in 1581, and a tenth laird in Lanarkshire. Family details help to illustrate the manners of a period, and assist in elucidating some obscure points of national history. The list of members of ancient Scottish Parliaments will, it is hoped, be found interesting, as well as the pictures of ancient Castles, for which I am indebted to the kindness of a proficient in Scottish archaeology and antiquities, Richard Gardiner, Esq., M.D.

Among the documents quoted are:-

MSS. in the Hotel des Archives, Paris.
The Register of the Great Seal.
The Register of the Privy Council.
The Register of the Lords in Council.
Acts and Decreets.
Acts of the Lords Auditors.
Register of Deeds.
Register of Retours.
Register of Wills.
Register of Sasines.
Register of the Privy Seal.
Horning Processes.
Justiciary Records.
Acts of the Scottish Parliament.
MSS. State Papers, London Record Office.
Maxwell Charters.
Book of Carlaverock.

Cott. MSS., British Museum, &c.
Holinshed's History of Scotland, 1577.
Dumfries Sasines.
Dumfries Registers.
Woodrow MSS.
The Mansfield Charter Chest.
The Galabank Charter Chest.
Wormanbie Charters.
MSS. from Lord Herries's Charter Chest.
Crawford's Peerage, 1716.
Nesbitt's Peerage, 1722.
Douglas's Peerage, 1761.
Fishing Acts, 1772.
Annan and Lochmaben Registers.
Hawick Charters.
History of the Carliles.

Lochmaben Castle

Chapter One

The conquest of England by the Romans [I think should mean the Normans] in 1066 brought a host of adventurers into the country, who were often rewarded for their part in the battle of Hastings by the sequestrated estates of the Saxon lords. Among these were Robert de Bruis, Jardine, Comyn, Pierre de Bailleul, Seigneur de Fescamps, and Le Seigneur de Jeanville, all mentioned by the Norman chronicler; and the three first were transferred to lands in the north of England. Cumberland and Lothian were claimed by both the English and the Scots at that time. Bruis or Bruce and Cumyn through marriages, and the others probably in a similar way, obtained a footing in Dumfriesshire, where the warlike character of the natives is still shown by the traces of Roman fortresses and encampments built along the Borders in early ages to oppose their advance upon South Britain. Here the Norman settlers intermarried with the Maxwells, Murrays, Carlyles, Kirkpatricks, Crichtons, Carrutherses, Irvings, Grahames, Griersons, Fergussons, and other families in Annandale, who, after Cumberland finally became English, formed an effectual barrier against any further encroachments from the south.

The rivers Esk and Sark, and a morass called Solway Moss, make a natural boundary between Cumberland and Dumfriesshire, added to the bleak tract of country extending for about seven miles from the mouth of the Annan to the Sark. The deep valley of the Annan and the banks of the Milk, with their isolated towns and villages, occasionally recall Switzerland to the modern tourist, and before the union of the two crowns were favourite hiding places for outlaws and bandits, as the arm of the law had difficulty in penetrating to these remote regions, except through the chiefs of the clans. The English borderers were as rude and nearly as aggressive as their Scottish neighbours, so that peace never existed long between North Cumberland and South Dumfriesshire, whatever treaties were signed by their respective kings. Gretna or Graitney, Annan, Newbie, Sark or Morton, Caerlaverock, Holmains, Dunskellie (now Cove), Lochwood, Hoddam, Johnstone, Closeburn or Killosburn, Amisfield, and Comlongan all possessed fortified towers, where the owners occasionally withstood a siege. The Castle of Lochmaben, which the King retained in his own hands, had walls eight feet in thickness, and the sovereigns occasionally made it their temporary residence.

Early in the 12th century, Robert de Bruis or Bruce held the title of Lord of the Valley of Annan or Annandale, besides large estates in Yorkshire, where he founded the monastery of Gysburn. He gave to this house the patronage of all the churches in Annandale, and his son and grandson, William and Robert, confirmed the gift. The original deeds, preserved at York, are signed, among others, by Humphrey de Gardine (Jardine) and Adam Carlile, both well-known border names, and the churches, described are Lochmaben, Kirkpatrick, Cumbertrees, Rein Patrik (now Redkirk), Gretenhow (or Gretna), and Annan. In the subsequent wars between England and Scotland these churches were made over to the See of Glasgow, and long before the Reformation were generally sold to lay patrons. Between 1170 and 1180 William de Bruce, Lord of Annandale, granted lands to Adam Carlyle, a native of the soil who held property in Cumberland, and the lands of Newbie in Dumfriesshire; and in a charter of Henry de Graeme, ancestor of the Duke of Montrose, the district of Dumfriesshire from Wamphray, inclusive, to Greistna Grene is granted to David Carlyle, Lord of Torthorwald. These early charters have no dates, which can only be ascertained by the reign of the King of Scotland under whom they were conferred. "Twa score Carvels (Carlyles) frae Cockpool" are mentioned in an ancient ballad called "The Bedesman of Nithsdale" as having followed Richard I. of England to the Crusades.

The pedigree of the Bruces goes back into the regions of fable. As Princes of Orkney and Caithness, they had a connection with Scotland in the 9th century, and their chief married the daughter of Malcolm II. of Scotland. His son, Regenwald, a sea king, roved through Europe for a bride, and found one in the daughter of Vladimir the Great, the first Christian Czar of Russia. Regenwald finally settled in Normandy, and his grandson Robert followed the fortunes of the Conqueror. His descendant Robert Bruce, Lord of Annandale, married the natural daughter of the Scottish King, William, who, following the example of his son-in-law (up to that time Scotland was without a coat of arms), assumed a heraldic distinction, and bore a lion on his shield. The son of this Bruce espoused King William's niece, and was the father of the Lord of Annandale, known as the competitor for the throne of Scotland in 1286. Another branch of the family remained in England, where it still exists; while the house of Robert the First became extinct in the male line with his only son David II., for his four brothers, all slaughtered during the long war with England, had died childless. His daughter Marjory died before her father, but she had married Walter, son of James, High Steward of Scotland, and was the ancestress of the Stuarts or Stewards, and of her gracious Majesty.

6

Robert Bruce, the son of the competitor and father of the great Bruce, seems to have been English in his sympathies, and had formed a second marriage with the daughter of Edward's ally, the Earl of Ulster. It was not till he died that his son (who had received a pardon from Edward I. for killing a stag in the King's English forests) took an ostensible part on the side of Scotland. The elder Bruce had fought with Edward I. and with Louis IX. in the Holy Land, and it is probable that one of the family, like the Carliles, also accompanied Richard I. to the Crusades, for the Jardines, Johnstones, and Kirkpatricks carry the same saltire and chief as the Bruces on their shields, and it is believed that they adopted them when fighting with the Lord of Annandale against the Saracens..

With the Bruces and Baliols, the Graemes or Grahames, Carliles, and Corries, seem at this date to have been the chief landowners in Dumfriesshire. The Grahames and Carliles claimed direct descent—the first from King Grime, and the last from Malcolm II. of Scotland; and with their kindred, the Kirkpatricks, were on good terms apparently with the Norman immigrants, as their names are frequently found together on inquisitions, or as witnesses to the same deeds. Two of the sisters of the great Bruce married Annandale men, Sir Christopher Seton and Sir William de Carlile, and the wife of Carlile left numerous descendants. But the Carlile property, which once comprised half of Annandale, was reduced in 1700 to a few isolated estates; and no Carlile appears as a Member of Parliament for any part of Dumfriesshire after 1357.

Holywood Church

The Lord Carlile who supped with Bothwell in 1567, on the eve of the murder of King Henry, could not sign his own name.

The second son of Sir William de Carlile and Margaret Bruce was killed at the battle of Durham in 1346, leaving one child, Susanna, who was afterwards married to Robert Corrie. A charter in favour of his brother William de Carlile from Robert Bruce styles him the King's sister's son; and another dated at Melrose, 1363, from David II. in favour of Susanna Carlile and of her husband, Robert Corrie, calls the deceased Thomas Carlile the King's blood relation, and grants to his daughter and her spouse the lands along the southern coast of Dumfriesshire, which had belonged to her grandfather. The Corries (the name is Celtic for hollow) were the hereditary keepers of the castle of Loch Doon in 1306, and a little later, owing to the marriage above-named, added greatly to their possessions in Dumfriesshire. Besides the Barony of Corrie, comprising the modern parishes of Hutton and Corrie, they owned Keldwood in the modern Cumberland parish of Kirkandrews-upon-Esk, Comlongan, Ruthwell, the Barony of Newbie, the Barony of Stapleton, Robgill, and part of the parish of St. Patrick, now divided into Kirkpatrick-Fleming; and Gretna, which includes the ruins of the ancient Redkirk or Rampatrick, and the celebrated Lochmaben Stone, where treaties were signed with the English. But during the 15th century the rebellion of the Douglases involved Dumfriesshire in a civil war. In 1484 George Corrie took the side of the insurgents against the King, and when they were defeated he was outlawed, and part of his estates transferred to Thomas Carruthers, a loyal freeman in Annandale. His brothers, Thomas and William Corrie, for some time retained a portion of the family lands, but subject to constant forays on the part of their neighbours, and in spite of numerous lawsuits, they could get no redress. Yet Thomas Corrie of Kelwood and Newbie was of sufficient importance to be appointed in 1529, with the King's treasurer and two Scottish knights, an arbiter in a family matter between the Earls of Eglintoun and Glencairn. He married a daughter of Lord Herries.

Dumfriesshire supplied many soldiers for the service of Sir William Wallace, who called himself guardian of the kingdom for King John; and as Lord of Annan, Baliol [Baliol's father was buried in 1269 at Sweetheart Abbey near Dumfries, which had been founded by his wife Devongilla, daughter of Allan, Lord of Galloway. She also founded Holywood, and built the Old Bridge at Dumfries.] seems to have had his strongest support in Annandale. Lochmaben, Sanquhar, Caerlaverock, Graitney, and Annan changed hands very frequently between 1296 and 1370, and in the middle of the present century an inscription was still legible on a tomb in Graitney Churchyard showing that it belonged to a near relative of Wallace.

Note.—Hostages for the Ransom of David II., 1357.—"John Steward (Robt. III.); Humphrey Kirkpatrick; Reynald, son and heir of Sir J. More; Gilbert, ditto of John Kennedy; John, ditto of John Berkeley; John Fleming, son of the Earl of Wigton; John, son of Andrea de Valence; Patrick, son of Sir David Graham; Robt., son of Sir Wm. Cunningham; Robt., son of Sir John Steward of Darnley; Robt., son and heir of Sir Robt. Darzel; Thos., son to Robt. Esk; Wm., son of Thos. Somerville; David, son of David de Wemyss; Thos., son of Wm. de la Haye of Loughewode; John, son and heir to John Gray; John, son and heir of the Earl of Sutherland, is sent to London with his father to appear before the Chancellor; Wm., son and heir to the Earl of Rosse, is sick, and King David and the Bishops of St. Andrew, Brechin, and the Earl of March have undertaken that he shall be delivered if he is alive to the Keeper of Berwick before Easter, and if he be dead, that the next heir of the said Earl shall come in his place."

—(Original MS. in London Record Office.)

Chapter Two

So late as the reign of Alexander III. (died 1286) the district extending from the Solway to the Clyde was still known as Cumbria, or the land of the Celts; while the country between Northumbria and the Forth was called Saxony, from the number of English immigrants who had sought a refuge there when William the Conqueror laid waste the district north of the Humber. In Cumbria Christianity was introduced from Iona before it had been embraced by the Saxons of South Britain. St. Ninian, from Rome, built a church in Galloway in 412, and that long stood alone, but the Irish St. Colomba and his followers had settled at Iona, and were active missionaries in Dumfriesshire in the 6th century. "Tis plain," says Maitland, one of the first authorities on early Scottish history, "that the Christian Scots were converted before the arrival of Palladius, the first bishop, by persons of a different communion to the Church of Rome, as is manifest by the disputes afterwards carried on by Coleman and other Scottish chiefs against the followers of Austin the Monk (St. Augustine) concerning the keeping of Easter, which by its being kept by the Scots according to the practice of the Eastern Church shows that our ancestors, instead of being proselytized by the Church of Rome, owed their conversion to the Greek Church, as no doubt the Britons did, by their maintaining the same doctrine." Soul's Seat or Salsit, in Galloway, was always admitted to be a non Roman ecclesiastical house. As the Danes and Norwegians possessed the Hebrides, the Isle of Man, and some authority over Argyllshire, it is probable that they had a footing in Dumfriesshire. By or Bie, a Norse termination, is found to several Dumfries names; and the ancient runic cross at Ruthwell, adorned with Christian symbols, is similar to another erected at Campbeltown in Argyll, and they are the only two remaining in Scotland. The names of Bridekirk, Kirkpatrick, Redkirk or Rampatrick come from Irish saints. St. Mungo is also Celtic; and the Roriesons anglicized their appellation from MacRorie, its original form (borne by the Lords of Bute), as did the Thomsons, Fergussons, Andersons, and some other families with the termination son.

The Greek, rather than Roman, source from which the Columba Christians derived their faith perhaps accounts for the prevalence of Greek Christian names in the earliest records of Dumfriesshire. Agamemnon, Homer, Achilles, Michael, Hercules, Constantine, Simon, Alexander, Andreas, Nicolas (for both men and women), Helen, Agnes, Catherine, Sapientia, and many more frequently appear. Chalmers has conjectured that all the Norman families found in Annandale in the 13th century were invited to settle there by David I., who, as Earl of Cumberland, had been companion in arms with Robert Bruce at the Court of Henry I. This Robert Bruce was probably the same who came over with William the Conqueror or his son, and he appears as a witness in deeds connected with Henry I. Robert de Comyn (the same as the French Comines) was made Earl of Northumberland, and was killed at the siege of Alnwick in

1093. Malcolm Canmore, King of Scotland, who was killed on the same occasion, did homage to England for the county of Cumberland, then united to Dumfriesshire, a wild and uncontrolled part of Scotland; and his son David having seen the superior refinement of the Norman French knights to those of England and Scotland, hoped by their means to civilize the natives of Cumbria, who were much the same as the wild Scots or Galwegians. The crusades brought the military of all nations together on the fields of Palestine, and made them acquainted with each other's characteristics. Like Malcolm III., Alexander III. did homage to the English King, his brother-in-law, for Cumberland; and everything prophesied the closest relations in the future between the two countries, when a series of premature deaths, and what some call the unprincipled ambition, others the high policy of Edward I., inaugurated a long war, and all its consequent miseries. The misfortunes of Scotland towards the close of the reign of Alexander III. began with the death of the King's younger son David in 1281. In 1283 the elder son, Alexander, Prince of Scotland, also died, and a letter from Sir Raoul Fleming to the King of England requested a safe conduct for himself and the Sieur de Baliol, as well as for "their young lady," widow of the Prince, through England, on her way back to her father's Court in Flanders. On February 5, the Scottish nobles had recognised Margaret, daughter of the late Margaret, Princess of Scotland, by her marriage with Eric, King of Norway, as their future Queen, and Edward lost no time in obtaining, with much expense, a dispensation from the Pope for his own son to marry within the prohibited degrees, with a view to a future wedding between this youthful heiress and the Prince of Wales.

A letter from Alexander III. to Edward, in April of the same year, thanks the King for a long course of benefits, and for his sympathy transmitted by his messenger, Friar John of St. Germains, which afforded him great solace in these intolerable difficulties and troubles which he has sustained, and still feels, through the death of his most beloved son, the King's dearest nephew. [From the Scottish Chronicles collected in the London Record Office edited by Joseph Bain, F.S.A.] Though death had carried off all his blood in Scotland, yet one remained, the child of his own dearest daughter, King Edward's niece, and now, under Divine Providence, the heir apparent of Scotland. Much good may yet be in store for them, and death only can dissolve their league of unity. He requests a reply through his messenger, Andrew Abbot of Cupar. The letter is dated Edinburgh Castle, 20th April, and 35th of his reign.

A letter to Edward I. from this young Prince Alexander is still extant. He styles himself the English King's "own nephew, and first-born son of Alexander, King of Scotland, to his most hearty uncle the King," and expresses the warmest affection for himself, the Queen, and their children, and wishes to hear of them more frequently. He believes the King will be glad to hear good news of himself and his kindred, and as he has no seal of his own (he was but sixteen) he uses that of Sir W. de Saint Clair, his guardian. His sister also wrote a year later to the King, telling him that she is "healthy and lively by God's mercy, and hopes he will constantly inform her of his own state which

God keep, and of his wishes towards her." She seals with the seal of Dame Luce de Hessewell, her chamberer—lady of the bed-chamber—and concludes with a thousand salutations. The Armstrongs were even then beginning to give trouble. One named John had been killed by James de Multon, for whom Alexander III. solicits a pardon from his brother-in-law, 1281.

The Scottish King re-married after the death of his son, but within a year was killed by a fall from his horse over, a cliff in Fifeshire at the age of 44, and with him ended the line of the native Celtic kings. Edward I. at once lent the King of Norway, father of the infant Queen, 2000 marks to bring her to Scotland, and granted annuities to several Norwegians of rank; but the child died, possibly of sea sickness, in Orkney, before she had touched the Scottish shore, and while Edward was fitting out a great vessel at Hull to bring "Margaret, the damsel of Scotland," to England. The Bishop of St. Andrews wrote to beg him to come to the Borders to prevent disorders, for the Lord of Annandale (Robert Bruce, the grandfather) had unexpectedly arrived with a formidable retinue at Perth, and with eleven other competitors was prepared to dispute the crown. The claims of nine were soon dismissed, and of the pretensions of John Baliol, Lord of Galloway and Annan, of John Comyn, Lord of Badenoch, and of Robert Bruce, Edward I. gave the casting vote in favour of Baliol, as descended from the eldest female branch, but on conditions which destroyed the independence of Scotland, as they included the maintenance of English garrisons in all the principal fortresses, and the performance by Baliol of homage to Edward for all his Scottish provinces.

Comyn renounced his own claim to support that of Baliol, his brother-in-law, and was appointed to

Torthorwald

high office by Edward I. All the Scottish noblemen except William Douglas took an oath of fidelity for themselves and their heirs in the most solemn terms to Edward at Roxburgh, Berwick-upon-Tweed, and other Scottish towns in 1296, and the documents which record it, with their names and seals attached, called the Ragman's Roll, are still preserved. With the exception of the Bruces, the Dumfriesshire lairds seem generally to have kept the oath. Dumfriesshire was indeed held by the English till the disadvantageous peace with Scotland, made during the minority of Edward III., and which an old English writer treats as a judgment on England for the murder of Edward II.; and the Baillies, Cathcarts, Craigies, Gordons, Grahames, Kirkpatricks, Setons, [With the Setons fear must have been the motive, for the father of Bruce's brother-in-law was hung, drawn, and quartered by the English. The men of Galloway, descended from the wild Scots who inhabited the Highlands and borders of Dumfriesshire, are said to have thrown off their clothes when they went into battle. Speed depicts them as wearing nothing but a blanket or plaid wrapped round them, and held together by the hand like an Arab's burnoose. The women wore the same garment, but made a hood of it.] St. Clairs, Stewards of Bonkill, Carliles of Torthorwald, and others, particularly Annandale men, fought for the English long after the death of Edward I.

In the civil wars occasioned by the arrival on Scottish soil of Prince James Stuart in 1715, and of Prince Charles Edward in 1745, some members of a family adhered to the cause of King George, while the rest took up arms for his opponent in order to save the family property, and probably this was the case in the time of the Plantagents. Even the horrible penalties for high treason inflicted in England so late as 1745, and which were carried out most illegally (and apparently introduced) under Edward I. (the Scots not being his subjects could not be accused of high treason) did not deter some of those most likely to fall into English hands from taking up arms for Robert Bruce. The Earl of Ulster, related to both Bruce and the Stewards of Scotland, gave his support to Edward I. Robert Bruce effected an alliance with the native princes of Wales and with part of Ireland, and in time many of the lairds of Celtic descent joined his standard. Of Norman origin, it was natural that with those Scottish chiefs of Norman descent he should at first adhere to Edward I., and it was not till he was excommunicated by the Pope, and outlawed by the civil power for the death of Comyn in the chancel of the Grey Friars' Church at Dumfries, that he openly assumed the role of a Scottish patriot. Almost the last of Edward's acts was to order the execution of Thomas and Alexander Bruce, who had been taken prisoners in Galloway as they were marching at the head of some Irish forces to join their brother. Although desperately wounded they were carried actually bleeding on to the scaffold at Carlisle (February 9, 1307). Three months before, their brother Nigel Bruce, had been hung, drawn, and quartered at Perth by order of the English governor; and the Countess of Buchan, with King Robert's daughter Marjory, his second wife, the Countess of Carrick (as she was called), and his sisters, Christine and Marie, who was afterwards exchanged for Walter Comyn, and married Sir Nigel Campbell, the ancestor of the Duke of Argyle, were all dragged out of the sanctuary of St. Duthoc at Tain, where they had taken refuge, and three of the ladies, including Bruce's sisters, were imprisoned in cages. In February, 1314, King Robert's wife was in prison at Rochester Castle. Edward II., then reigning, seems to have been very humane with regard to the Scottish prisoners, and he ordered her at that time to have "a sufficient chamber," and 20s a week for expenses. She was also to be allowed exercise within the Castle and St. Andrew's Priory at suitable times. A year later she was exchanged with her sister-in-law, Christine, her stepdaughter, Marjory, her brother-in-law, the Earl of Mar, and the Bishop of Glasgow for some of the English prisoners captured at the battle of Bannockburn.

In later days nearly every Scottish family has tried to show that its ancestors was on the side of Bruce or Wallace, but unfortunately this cannot be proved. The appeal by the Scottish nobles to the Pope stating the proofs that Scotland had a right to be independent, alleged truly enough that the signatures to the Ragman's Roll had been obtained by the "threats and horrid tortures" to which Edward had subjected all who opposed him. It stated that the Scottish nation (Speed, in the reign of Elizabeth, derives the name of the Scots from Scyth) issuing out of greater Scythia, passed the Tyrenian Sea and the pillars of Hercules, and for a long time resided in Spain. (In Speed's days Cape Finisterre was called Scythicus in remembrance of their sojourn in Spain.) There, said the memorial, they could not be subdued, though among a very fierce people, and they had eventually found their way to the west of Scotland, where they expelled the Britons and destroyed the aborigines, maintaining themselves against the invasions of Danes, Norwegians, and English. This was dated from Aberbrothock, 1320. Undoubtedly the Scots would have earlier shaken off the English yoke if there had not been divisions among their leading men. It was the attitude of the Scottish nobles, including Bruce and Comyn, that caused the defeat of Wallace; and Sir John Steward of Menteith, who betrayed the popular hero to the English, was on friendly terms with Bruce, and great-uncle to his son-in-law. The temporalities of the bishopric of Glasgow, in Annandale, were granted to Sir John Steward for "great services" by Edward I. in 1306. These great services were the betrayal of Wallace, though Sir John has apologists who try to prove his innocence in the matter. Sir William Carlile, King Robert's brother-in-law, did not join the Scots till 1317. He then forfeited his lands in Cumberland, but as his sons William and John, and his brothers Thomas and James, all adhered to England, it is probable that the descendants of one or other of them obtained the restoration of the lands of Newbie in Cumberland, which bore the same name as the paternal inheritance in Dumfriesshire. In later centuries there were English Carliles of some distinction who claimed an origin from the owners of Newbie in Cumberland. In the State accounts of Edward II., Sir Thomas de Torthorald — i.e., Carlile of Torthorald—is described as being killed in the English Warden's raid on the Scots near Redcross, November 30, 1314. The same year Johanna, widow of Sir James de Torthorald, killed in the King's service at Stirling, writes to acknowledge 8 qrs. of wheat and 10 qrs. of beans and pease sent to her from the King's stores "for the sustenance of herself and her children." She appends her seal to the letter, and a little later was granted an annuity. On the 24th of July, 1347, an inquisition, held at Lochmaben under a writ of the Duchy of Lancaster, by Gilbert de Joneston, Wm. de Levyngton, Robt. de Crosby, Adam Latimer, Thos. de la Beck, Wm. Mounceux, Robert son of John, Wm. del Lathes, Nicolas del Skaleby, Adam del Yate, and Helias Post, jurors, declared William de Carlile to be the son and heir of the late John de Carlile (second son of Sir William de Carlile and Lady Marjory Bruce), and nearest heir to his uncle William de Carlile. They further show that the late William did nothing against his lord (the English King) at any time; nor did William, son and heir of the late John de Carlile, that he should not recover his lands of Luce, in the Burgh of Annan, Loughwode, Woodhouse, &c. Throughout his career Bruce was remarkable for his magnanimity towards his enemies, and even towards his faithless friends; and the same quality was not absent in his son David, nor in their opponents, Edward II. and III. The difficult position of Dumfriesshire lairds was evidently taken into consideration by the Scottish and English Monarchs, for Thomas de Torthorald, the second son of Sir W. de Carlile and Marjory Bruce, had been killed the previous year at the battle of Durham when fighting by the side of David II. The head of the family in 1431 married Elizabeth Kirkpatrick. Their grandson, Alexander Carlile, second son of the first Lord Carlile of Torthorald, received Bridekirk as his portion, and his direct male descendant, John, son of Thomas, son of Alexander Carlile of Bridekirk, had a charter of the ecclesiastical lands of Torthorald in 1605 as one of the male heirs of the original grantee. Robert Carlile, laird of Bridekirk, was one of the nearest of kin who took out letters of slain for the murder of James Douglas, Lord of Torthorald, who had married the heiress of the Carlile barony, and when he "was walking in peaceable and quiet manner," as the indictment set forth, "upon the High Street of the Burgh of Edinburgh, looking for nothing less than any trouble, pursuit, or injury against him"(14th July, 1608), was stabbed by William Stewart, whose father, Captain James Stewart, had been killed by Douglas in 1596. The relatives on each side were ordered to find caution for keeping the peace, as "His Majesty (James VI.) cannot abide," [In spite of this objection by James VI. the practice was evidently in full force in Dumfriesshire in 1628.] says the legal document, "the reviving of that ugly monster of deadly feud, and will take care that justice is administered in the matter if the said pursuers will challenge Lord Ochiltree (Stewart) as guilty of the said slaughter."

But to return to earlier times. The seizure by Edward I. of all Scottish deeds and charters deposited at Perth, Lochmaben, and other towns held by his garrisons, afforded room for much imagination with regard to some of the Scottish family histories. The ancestor of the Grahames who broke through the wall of Severus in the 5th century, the descent of the Kirkpatricks from Fingal, and of the Stewarts from Banquo, could hardly be proved in a court of law. The Stuart Celtic pedigree is found in the visitation of Notts as early as 1611, but is demolished by Lord Hailes; and the charters of grants of lands made by members of the family to St. Peter's Cathedral at York, prior to the days of Bruce, [Among the early grants to the hospital of St. Peter of York, Walter Fitzalan, Steward of the King of Scotland, grants two pieces of land and a common pasture for the souls of King David and Malcolm, and of his parents and predecessors, and for the present weal of King William. Alan, son of Walter, Steward of Scotland, witnesses a charter for King Malcolm. Eudo de Carlile, son of Adam, son of Robert, also grants an estate in Dumfriesshire.] show

14

their Norman origin. The last Celtic Kings of Scotland resisted the claim of the Sees of York and Canterbury to have any authority over Scottish churchmen. The Stewarts are declared by the best chroniclers to be descendants of Fitz-Alleyne, one of the companions of William the Conqueror, who was killed at Hastings. His relative Alan obtained from William the barony of Oswestry, in Shropshire, and possibly one of the family may have married Nesta, the daughter of Griffith, Prince of Wales, as the pedigree alleges, considering their near neighbourhood, but there is no proof of it. There is also no documentary proof that Oliver Cromwell had any connection with the royal house of Stuart, as has been alleged, but Charles Stuart, a grandson of the Prior of Coldinghame, half-brother to Queen Mary, did bear arms against Charles I. Many interloping Saxon families on the estates of Celtic lairds are said to have adopted their predecessors' names and pedigrees. But a love of over-long pedigrees was always characteristic of Scotland. At the coronation of Alexander III. an ancient Herald enumerated his alleged ancestors, fifty-six in number, from the first Scottish King, and as far back as one of the Pharoahs.

It is supposed that after swearing fealty to Edward I. and his heirs for ever in 1296, and also after the elder Bruce had been infefted in the lands which his father had owned in several parts of England, Robert Bruce, the younger, and the Steward family were impressed with the successes of Sir William Wallace and his followers, and made overtures to join him. It must be owned that their conduct at this period is very obscure. Blind Harry the minstrel is really our chief authority for the career of William Wallace. The English contemporary records scarcely allude to his exploits, but state that his two brothers surrendered to the English governor at Perth, and were at once hung, drawn, and quartered. The Scottish writers under the Stuart dynasty naturally attributed patriotism to the fathers of their Kings, throughout these almost civil wars, in the same way that they gave them a Celtic ancestry, which Shakespeare has introduced into ordinary history; but the English records relate that on July 9, 1297, "Robert de Brus, Earl of Carrick, James, the Steward of Scotland, and John, the brother of the Steward, confess their rebellion against the King (Edward), and place themselves in his will." This John is supposed to have been John Steward of Bonkill, who is reported to have been killed at the battle of Falkirk a year later fighting for Scotland. Old pedigrees made him out to be the father of Walter the Steward, who married Marjory Bruce, though Walter's father is now generally acknowledged to have been James the Steward, who married Egidia de Burgh; but is there evidence beyond that of courtly writers (who perhaps like those in Austria at the present day were liable to a penalty and the suppression of their books if they wrote any ill of the monarch's predecessors) that John Steward of Bonkill was killed on the side of Wallace? He was certainly alone among his kindred if he assisted the so-called lieutenant of King John Baliol, who signed all his orders in the name of Bruce's rival. Baliol was brought to England and detained there in 1296 in consequence of some of the Scottish nobles having persuaded him to conclude an offensive and defensive alliance with France when at war with

England, and Wallace's rising was to accomplish the object contemplated by that affiance, the expulsion of the English garrisons from Scotland. If he had declared for the younger Bruce, whose family for four generations had looked upon themselves as probable inheritors of the throne, he might have obtained the full support of the Stewards and Bruces, who were cousins through the mother of Robert I., as well as connected by marriages with the Anglo-Irish de Burghs. At the request of Edward III., when peace was temporarily effected in 1328, Sir John de Carlile of Torthorald was restored to his property in Dumfriesshire. Sir Roger de Kirkpatrick, the murderer of Comyn (Baliol's nephew), seems to have deserted Robert Bruce as early as 1315, when we hear of him as commander of Lochmaben Castle (which had surrendered to Edward II., when Prince of Wales, in 1306) holding it for the King of England. He received as pay for himself and four esquires £4 16s 0d for twelve days. At the same time and place Sir William Heriz and his esquire were paid 36s; Sir Thomas de Torthorald, knight, and his esquire, 36s; the esquire Alan de Dunwithie, with his valet and steed, 12s; Sir Robert the chaplain, 7s; Henry de Carlile, a cross-bowman, 6d; and others in proportion. After the battle of Falkirk, gained by the English over Wallace, these Scotsmen received compensation for their slain horses at the following rates:—Sir Roger de Kirkpatrick received for a brown bay £10; Sir James de Carlile, £10; William Comyn, of the King's son's household, 100s; Sir Humphrey de Jardine had only 12 marks for a black horse with two white feet and star on its forehead; Sir Thomas de Carlile lost one worth 100s; and William de Gardin's valet's horse was valued at 6 marks.

The murderer of Comyn had been excommunicated by the Pope, and his end seems never to have been ascertained. After serving Edward I., who appointed him a justice of the peace, he turned to Bruce, yet was serving Edward in 1315, and apparently again joined Bruce, for after King Robert's fortunes seemed declining, and he was known to be afflicted with leprosy, so that there was every prospect of a minor sovereign and all the evils it would entail, Sir Roger Kirkpatrick and his wife asked for a safe conduct and protection within the realm of England. The same was asked for a year for Humfrey de Kirkpatrick and Idonia his wife, December 12, 1322. Seven weeks later King Edward II. ordered instant inquiry to be made by good men of Cumberland and Westmoreland as to the abduction of Sir Roger Kirkpatrick, Knight of Scotland, and his wife, who fled to England to save his life, and while there, under the King's special protection, have been seized by evil-doers, and are still detained in some place unknown. This order is dated from York, and as seven months later another to the same effect is dated from Berwick-upon-Tweed, and there is no further mention of them, they were probably secretly murdered by some of Comyn's friends. In 1341 Humphrey Kirkpatrick, son and heir of Roger Kirkpatrick, was one of seventeen hostages for the ransom of David II., who were sent to England; another being John Fernyear or Stewart, afterwards Robert III.

A Humfrey de Kirkpatrick was a witness to a grant of the lands and advowson of Ecclefechan to Sir Robert Bruce and his heirs in 1249. The other witnesses are Sir Walter Comyn, Earl of Menteith, Sir A. Cummin, Earl of Buchan, Sir John Cummin, Sir William de Cunnynghame, Hugh de Mauleverer, Gilbert de Johnestoun, Ivo de Jonesby, Richard de Crossbie, William de Boyville, William de Annaud, clerk, and others. This is the first time in which a descendant of Le Seigneur de Jeanville or Joinville—the name was spelt both ways in France—is mentioned in Dumfriesshire records as Johnestoun [Archibald Johnstone of Warriestoun, executed in 1662, signed his name Johnstown.] or Johnstone, for it appears in the original French in a deed connected with the Carlile family, signed by Gulielmo de Joyneville, as late as between 1191 and 1215. The barony of Joinville, in the province of Champagne in France, passed in the 15th century into that of Lorraine. It was here, at the Castle of Joinville, that the French historian of the same name, who is described as a cadet of an ancient family in Champagne, was born in 1274, and was early introduced to the Comte de Thibaudeau at the French Court. He died in 1319, but was at the height of his popularity with King Philip le Bel when Geoffrey or Gilbert de Jeanville, [The deeds of this period and long afterwards were usually signed by a clerk for all the witnesses, who sometimes went through the form of putting their hands on the pen; but, as they could not read the deeds when they were written, mistakes are often found in places and Christian names. In a Scottish Crown Charter of 1517 the same man is first called Herbert then Gilbert. In a decreet of the Privy Council in 1591 Edward Johnstone of Ryehill is called Andrew. In other registered Scottish deeds John is called James; Peter is called Patrick; Ryhill, Robgill; Marion, Margaret; and the second Marquis of Annandale and Earl of Hartfell is called Earl of Hertford, even in the Register of Burials in Westminster Abbey in 1730. Gilbert and Geoffrey are more than once transposed, and this Jeanville is called both in copies of the deed.] known in Dumfriesshire as Johnestoune, an adherent of Baliol, came in 1299 with the English Commissioners to sign a treaty between Edward I. and the Scottish King John with King Philip of France, which had been arranged through the medium of the Pope. The treaty was signed for the Pope by Bishop Kenault of Vicenza, and for England by John of Winchester, Symon of Salisbury, Bishop Aymer de Savoie, Henry de Nicolas Guis de Warwick, Count Aymer dc Valence, Otto de Granson, John of Bar Chevalier, and Geoffrey or Guilbert de Jeanville, and there can be little doubt that the last was of the same family as Philip's historiographer, and that it was from the Joinville or Jeanville barony that the Seigneur de Jeanville, mentioned by the old chronicler Guilliaume de Tailleur as being with William's army among princes and nobles from Germany, and distant parts of France, came to join the Conqueror's forces before the battle of Hastings, and half Saxonized into Janvil, the name appears again on the roll of Battle Abbey. Like other Norman French families planted in Scotland, the Johnstones obtained estates in different parts of the country, but the manor, if not the advowson, of the Church of Johnstone was bestowed on the monastery of Soltray by Sir John de Johnstone about 1285, when he confirmed his father's (Hugo de Johnestoune) gift of the lands in Haddington to the same establishment. Soltray was particularly intended for the reception of pilgrims and strangers. It is difficult to find what other land the Johnstones owned so early as 1249, as most of the estates they afterwards held then belonged to the Bruces, Baliols, Corries, and Carliles. They may have held Graitney Tower, as Constables of the Borders, and Cavertholme, which was an early possession, for in1296 both Sir John de Johnstone and Gilbert Johnestoune are described as of Dumfriesshire. In 1333-4 a charter of lands in Annandale from Edward Baliol, calling himself King, to Henry Percy is signed by Gilbert de Johnstone of Brakenthwayte, an estate which was later held by the Carliles, and may have been exchanged with them, by marriage or other-wise, for Loughwode or Lochwood, which the Carliles held at that period (though it became later the stronghold of the lairds of Johnstone), because Brakenthwayte was never reclaimed by the Johnstones during the settlement of the Borders in 1603-20, when no title of possession seems to have been too obscure to be used. The other signatures to this charter of 1333-4 were— Adam de Corry, Keeper of the Castle of Lochmaben; Walter de Corry; Thomas de Kirkpatrick, in Penresax; William Kirkpatrick and the clerk, Thomas of Car-ruthers. Douglas states that Gilbert de Johnstone had a charter from Robert II. of lands in Lanarkshire, where Matthew de Johnstone of Westraw is found in 1455.

In the reign of David Bruce (1329-70), Stiven Johnstoune, whom his de-scendants affirm to have been described in their genealogies as brother to Johnstone, laird of Annandale, and a man of great learning, was in possession of the estate of Johnstone in Aberdeenshire, but his branch of the family adopted a different crest, though the same arms as the Johnstones in Dum-friesshire. It is curious that the seal attached to Sir John de Johnstoune's sig-nature (1296) to the Ragman's Roll has the coat of arms now borne by all his descendants, with the augmentations of mullets and garbs, only borne by the Johnstones of Galabank and Fulford Hall, while Gilbert de Johnstoune, who is supposed to have been his son, had on his seal a man on horseback, similar to that which was adopted as a distinctive crest by the illegitimate branch of the descendants of William Johnstone of Graitney and Baron of Newbie. Like the Maxwells, they adhered to England, instead of following the fortunes of Rob-ert Bruce. This may have been from loyalty or relationship to the Baliol fami-ly. King John Baliol's son, Edward, entered Dumfriesshire in 1332 with the aid, we are told, of the Anglo-Norman lords, whose Scottish lands had not been restored them, in spite of a clause in the Treaty of Peace, signed in 1327 between Robert Bruce and the Queen Regent of England. Probably most of the Border lairds assisted him, and a Charter, granting Ryvel and Comlongan to one of Baliol's supporters, Murray (ancestor of the Duke of Athol), is signed by John de Johnestoune and his son, Gilbert, as well as by Humfrie de Bosco and Roger de Kirkpatrick before 1331. Again, in 1347, Gilbert de Johnstone was presiding over the inquisition which returned young Carlile as heir to his uncle, under English auspices. In 1341 David Bruce invaded England during the absence of Edward III. in France, possibly with a view of obtaining the restoration of all Dumfriesshire. He was defeated, and taken prisoner into England; but Edward was just then more set upon the conquest of France than of England, and in 1356, owing to the capture of the fortified towns in Dumfriesshire, and the offer of a ransom for the young king by Robert Stuart, who ruled the country as Regent during his imprisonment, Edward Baliol retired, so that the Johnstones, Maxwells, and others were released from any further allegiance to his house. Sir John of Johnstone, the son of Gilbert, was made a Warden of the West Borders at this time, and Adam de Johnstone received a grant of the lands of Monyge, Moling, and Rahills. The old Prior of Lochleven, Andrew Wyntoun, who died about 1424, records, in the "Original Chronicle," the fame of Bruce, and of the Scottish leaders, his contemporaries. He gives a few lines to Sir John de Johnstone, who, in 1370, defeated the English army which invaded Scotland at the close of the reign of Edward III.:—

When att the wattyr of Solway,
Schyr Jhon of Jhonystown on a day,
Of Inglismen wencust a grete dele.
He bore him at that time sa wele
That he and the Lord of Gordoune,
Had a sowerane gude renown.
Of ony that was of thar degree
For full they war of grete bownte

Sir John Johnstone's son is mentioned in a letter from Robert II. (1385), in which the King thanks Charles VI. of France for the succour he has given him against the English, and for the sum of 40,000 livres which Charles had sent to be divided among "the Scottish nobles, his faithful allies." A list of the recipients is given, and among them John of Johnestoune had received 300 livres. He fought under Douglas at Otterburn or Chevy Chase, and was one of the constables (scutiferi) for keeping order on the Borders. In 1384 a safe conduct was obtained for him into England, wherein he is described as a military man. A large proportion of the Scotsmen, who asked for safe-conducts into England, either for trade or to go to the Continent, were Borderers. In 1413, one is obtained for Adam Johnstone, lord of Johnstone; Herbert, son and heir of Herbert Maxwell, lord of Caerlaverock; William Carlile, son and heir of John Carlile, soldier; Gilbert Grierson, Gilbert M'Dowall, son and heir of Fergus M'Dowall; and Archibald M'Dowall, soldier. In 1485, for Mr John Ireland, John Murray, David Scot, Gilbert de Johnstone, Lord Kennedy, David Lyle, Alex. Hume, &c. In March, 1464, a petition is presented from Adam of Johnstone, Robert and John Johnstone, Gilbert of Johnstone, and Matthew of Johnstone for several safe conducts for a whole year into England, with permission for two of them to trade at English ports with three boats of 15 tons burden, which boats have competent masters and mariners; also for the said petitioners to go freely between the two countries with ten Scotsmen in their company. Among the acts and decreets of this date in connection with a Borderer is one against Elizabeth, the widow of a certain James Burcane in Bruges, for detaining a pair of silver flagons, a stoup of silver gilt, a cup with a silver gilt cover, and a silver goblet left in her husband's care by John Lord Carlile.

While the English Kings appointed one wealthy English nobleman after another to the lordship of Annandale, Robert Bruce gave it to Sir James Douglas, who was attached to him not only by the ties of friendship, but by private wrongs sustained from Edward I. His father had aided Wallace, and then submitting to the English was imprisoned in the Tower of London, where he died, and his estates were forfeited, for besides his so-called rebellion he was the only Scotsman of rank who declined to sign the Ragman's Roll. James Douglas, then in France, came to Westminster, and offered to remain faithful to England if Edward would restore to him his father's lands. The King declined to give him either the lands or any employment, upon which he became a patriot, and joined Bruce. It is a well-known story that the name of his friend was changed from Lokarde to Lockhart, because he brought back Bruce's heart, which James Douglas had endeavoured to convey to the Holy Land; and the name of Lokard is found in Dumfriesshire as early as 1200. When the English were finally driven from Annandale the Douglases were for many years more powerful in this district than the Scottish King.

The Cars, Kers, and Kerrs, all one family, bear the same arms as the French branch of their house. They first settled in Teviotdale, at Ancrum, Fernihurst, and Cessford about 1330, but like the Hepburns of Bothwell, who are found in Berwickshire at the same period, they belong to the east frontier more than to Dumfriesshire. The Kerrs are now represented by the Duke of Roxburgh and the Marquis of Lothian. The eldest son of their house, Andrew Ker, was one of the hostages for the release of James I. In 1459 Andrew Ker of Cessford, John Johnstone of that ilk, Thos. Cranstoun of that ilk, George Ormiston, Charles Murray of Cockpool, William Carlile of Torthorald, and James Rutherford of that ilk are bracketted as "scutiferi," and as all "naval admirals," in the list of Border chiefs charged with the care of the marches. The same year David Hume, Walter Scott, Simon Glendinning, and Robert Crichton, Viscount of Nithsdale, were granted a safe conduct into England.

The Borderers are often compared to the Highlanders, who were of much the same race, in their system of clan-ship, but with the difference that they were all horsemen. The chief landowners were given baronial rights, which included the services of the freemen on their lands, whom they protected from each other and from the enemy. A code of unwritten laws existed, of which the origin is most obscure, but the object of the county courts, to judge from the cases tried, was to legislate between the families of the landowners, and to punish ill-doers among them. The peasantry could be dealt with in a more summary way. Their mode of life, as described by Froissart in 1323, was of the roughest description, but when we read that Bruce's army, which was all cavalry, contained a knight or esquire to every five troopers, its marvellous success is no matter of surprise. The "bold and hardy troopers armed after the manner of their country, and mounted on little hackneys that are never tied up or dressed, but turned immediately after the day's march to pasture on the heath or in the fields," brought no carts and carried no bread. "They can live on flesh, half sodden, without bread, and drink, the river water without wine. They dress the flesh of the cattle in their skins after they have flayed them. Under the flaps of his saddle each man carries a broad piece of metal behind him, with a little bag of oatmeal. When they have eaten too much of the sodden flesh, they set this plate over the fire, knead the meal with water, and make a thin cake of it, which they bake on the heated plate to warm their bodies." But in those times even the table of a Prince of Wales was not supplied with modern refinement. At Perth, Feb. 10, 1303-4, when the Prince, afterwards Edward II., gave a dinner to the King's envoys—Sir Aymer de Valence, Henry de Percy, Robert Fitz-Payn, and John de Beustede and their retinue "about the peace with Sir John Comyn"—the King's stores provided 1 shield of brawn, 100 herrings, 1 bushel of beans, 4 roes, 2 bushels of pease, 2 1/2 flagons of acetum, 1 flagon of verjuice, some bread, and 2 casks 6 sesterces of wine. From the Prince's store 11 bacons and 4 pieces of sturgeon. On Friday, Feb. 14, the Earl of Warwick and Sir Hugh le Despenser dined with the same Prince, on which occasion the King's stores supplied 1600 herrings, 44 stockfisb, 1 bushel of flour, 1 bushel of pease, 1/2 gallon of honey, 4 lbs. of anydoyne, 1/2 bushel of salt, 1/2 gallon of vinegar, two shillings worth of bread, and 62 sesterces of wine, and from the Prince's store were added 9 pieces of sturgeon.

An inquisition at Dumfries, April 23, 1347, held by John de la More, under sheriff (he was related to the first wife of Robert II.) to infeft Thos. de Molton in the whole manor of Kirkpatrick-Juxta, with the advowson of the Church and services of free men, is another instance of the early practice of giving benefices to laymen. Several Milners and Macaynes were the jurymen. Owing to the sequestrations and exactions by both the Scottish and English rulers, it was apparently difficult to find anything left but Church property with which to reward loyalty in Annandale. In 1297, Clifford had orders from Edward I. to occupy Bruce's estates in Annandale with his contingent, and in 1304 the escheats in other parts of Annandale amounted to £194 2s 6d, being £33 6s 3d for the relief of Walter de Corry, 60s 8d from the farm of the town of Annan, 19s 11d from toft mailes of the same town, 44s from the Provostry of Newbie, 44s 9 1/2d from the Provostry of Kirkpatrick and Gretna; 33s 4d from the mills of Moffatdale, £6 from the mill of Annan, and 6s from Loughwood.

The extraordinary efforts which Edward I. made to reduce Scotland to submission brought the greatest misfortunes on his son, and even affected the reign of his grandson. He had debased the coin to carry on his wars, and it was perfectly impossible to perform his two dying commands to pursue the war with Scotland and a crusade. The £30,000 he had left for the last purpose went to Hugh le Despenser and Piers de Gaveston to pay the dowry of their wives, £15,000 being the dowry of an English princess, and Despenser had married the sister and Gaveston the niece of Edward II. The country was impoverished and sick of the war, as is shown by the secret convention of the Earl of Carlisle with Robert Bruce, which cost the first his life and limbs. The terms offered by Robert Bruce—who even styles himself Sir, not King—were very liberal, and only to be explained by his already failing health. Among other things, if his title were acknowledged, he undertook to build an Abbey where daily mass should be celebrated for the souls of those who had perished in the long war. But Edward's last words still weighed on his son; while England was put to enormous expense in providing for the numerous Scottish prisoners, and the chiefs who still adhered to him. Complaints are recorded from all parts of the country as to the inability of the castellans and abbots to maintain them; even the once wealthy Prior of Gysburn points out that his monastery is ruined, and that he now gets nothing from Annandale and. Carlisle, which used to be the great source of his revenue; and this went on throughout the century. In 1376 the English officials cannot obtain the proper dues from Calfhirst (Cavertholme), Annan, Gretenhowe (Gretna), Kirkpatrick or Redkirk, for the tenants are ruined by the incursions of the Earl of March. In 1315 there had been a scarcity, and with the false political economy of the day, the English Parliament endeavoured to keep down prices, and ordered that a fatted ox should not cost more than 15s; a fat goose, 2 1/2d; a fat sheep, 1s 2d, and so on, till it became difficult to supply even the King's table, and the order was cancelled.

Sir Eustace de Maxwell received £22 yearly from Edward II. in 1312 for the defence of Caerlaverock, but he afterwards submitted to Robert Bruce, who razed its fortifications, and compensated him. It seems to have been rebuilt very soon, for the Earl of Northampton, then Sheriff of Annandale, tells an anonymous correspondent, in 1347, that Herbert de Maxwell had come to him in England to surrender the Castle of Caerlaverock under safe conduct from the King. He desires that no one on the English march should annoy him or his men, or take their victuals from them, and that he shall in all way be treated as an Englishman. In 1356, Caerlaverock was stormed by Roger Kirkpatrick, assisted by John, Earl of Carrick, afterwards Robert III., and Kirkpatrick was murdered the next year, in the middle of the night, by Sir James Lindsay, like himself a son of one of Comyn's murderers, and who was executed for it.

To an active Borderer, spending his life on horseback, close imprisonment in England was often fatal, but it was only those whose friends could provide a ransom who were thought worth capturing. An order in the handwriting of Edward III. commands the Warden of the Tower of London to receive from John de Clifford William de Gladestoun, chevalier, a Scottish prisoner, and keep him there. Westminster, 1357. The following year Thomas Gillisbe, Alexander Johnstone, James White, and John Roxburgh, imprisoned in Eccleshall Castle, Staffordshire, where they were allowed to go at large within the Castle, broke their parole, and escaped with their goods to the march between Scotland and England, where "they confederated with the lieges." An order was issued to re-imprison them, and deprive them of their goods. In 1422, John

Bell, James, William, John, and Walter Johnstone, Donald Brown, and others were released from the Tower, and allowed to return to Scotland to bring their ransoms. After depositing the money, they would be free to go back to Scotland.

Chapter Three

The misfortunes of the house of Stewart have become a proverb, but it must be admitted that in some measure their early Princes brought them on the dynasty by their own misdeeds. In the dispensation for his marriage to Elizabeth More within the prohibited degrees, obtained by Robert II. in 1347 from the Pope, both sons and daughters are mentioned who were probably legitimised by the matrimonial rite, but owing to his irregular life, both before and after the ceremony, it was commonly rumoured that though Robert III. was his eldest son, he was not one of the sons whose birth had been legalized by subsequent wedlock. The Duke of Albany was considered to have a better right to the throne, and his appointment as Regent in the life-time of his father, instead of his elder brother, seemed to confirm this report. The Wolf of Badenoch, another son of Robert II., was a ferocious savage; a destroyer of churches and monasteries for the sake of the silver they contained, and whose barbarities to women and children shocked even the rude clansman of his day. In spite of literary talent his nephew, James I., seemed to inherit a little of his cold cruelty, rather than the noble disposition of Robert Bruce. Great as had been his wrongs, and that of his elder brother, the treacherous seizure and execution of his cousin Murdoch—who had at one time shared his captivity in the Tower, obtained his release, and placed his crown on his head—and of Murdoch's sons and aged father-in-law after a mock trial, simply because the real sinner was dead, was regarded as an act of jealousy rather than of justice The horrible tortures to which he subjected some of their adherents, the insults heaped on his victims, and the confiscation of their possessions, chiefly for his own benefit, raised against him the faction of his and their relatives, who at last assassinated him, and his supplication for mercy when in the hands of his murderers contrasted with the stoical fortitude of the Albany family in their sufferings. By this revenge on descendants of the first wife of Robert II., James excited the indignation of the descendants of the second wife, Euphemia, *[Holinshead, writing in 1574, calls Euphemia Robert's first wife, and says he married Elizabeth Mure after her death, but he may have confused two rather similar names. Elizabeth's children legitimised after wedlock would have been junior in Scottish law to Euphemia's, though older in age.]* who also imagined that their right to reign, owing to their unquestioned legitimacy, was stronger than his own. These were the Earl of Atholl, Robert's son; his grandson, Stewart; and Sir Robert Grahame, a great grandson of Robert Bruce. But though ambition has been attributed to them, they asserted, amidst the excruciating torments to which they were subjected for their part in the King's death, by the order of his widow, the English Princess Joan, that they were simply avenging the blood of their relations by destroying the murderer according to the recognised Scottish law. While the Royal house was divided against itself, and the English Kings showed, by their detention of James I. in his boyhood (1399) in a time of peace and the ransom afterwards required for his release (1424), their continued ill-will to the Scots, the nobles on the borders and in the Highlands ruled independently of the Sovereigns, who when they visited Annandale came with an army as if entering foreign country.

A king of six years old, the heir of James I., was not likely to attract the allegiance of the powerful Douglas, whose predecessor had even claimed the throne, at the accession of the first Stewart. No mention can be found of the Douglases earlier than the last half of the 12th century, when William of Douglas witnessed a charter by Joscelin, Bishop of Glasgow, to the monks of Kelso, between 1170 and 1190. While the Maxwells devoted themselves to their relative Baliol, the Douglases adhered to Bruce. As lords of Galloway, Annandale, and Dumfries, they assumed an attitude very galling to the youthful sovereigns who inherited the Scottish throne. An inactive life soon wearied them, and when a truce was concluded with England, William, called the Black Douglas, who had married Egidia, or Gyles, the daughter of Robert II., left Scotland for a crusade against the pagans and fire-worshippers of Vilna in Russia, and enrolled himself under the flag of the Teutonic knights who had established themselves in Livonia and the north of modern Prussia. The Earl of Derby, afterwards Henry IV. of England, joined in the same expedition, and Douglas was made Admiral of the Teutonic fleet at Dantzic, Duke of Prussia, and Prince of Dantzic. He did not long enjoy these honours, for in 1400 he was murdered on the bridge of Dantzic by some assassins hired by Lord Clifford, one of the Earl of Derby's followers, with whom he had had a dispute. William, the nephew of this Douglas, when only seventeen years of age, kept a larger guard of armed followers than the young King, and excited the fears and jealousy of both the Regent and Sir William Crichton, the Chancellor of Scotland, who invited him and his young brother David to a banquet in the Royal Palace. In the middle of the feast they were seized and put to death by some of the Regent's servants, in the very sight of the Royal boy, "who grat very sore," writes the historian, and pleaded for their lives in vain. Yet a few years later their cousin and the head of their house was stabbed by this young King James II. in a fit of passion—an act which was the immediate cause of the great Douglas rebellion, that stirred up not only Dumfriesshire, but all Scotland, before it was finally suppressed.

The rebellion of the Earl of March in 1400, and of the Douglases fifty years later, made or ruined the fortunes of many families in Dumfriesshire. The Earl of March had been Warden of the Borders, and in that capacity had defeated the English and wrested the town of Roxburgh and the castle of Lochmaben from their hands; but he was incensed by the King's conduct to his daughter, Lady Elizabeth Dunbar, who after her betrothal to David, Prince of Scotland (the eldest son of Robert III.), with the Prince's full consent, and after her father had actually paid a large part of her promised dowry, was rejected for Lady Marjory, the daughter of the powerful Earl of Douglas, and Lady Marjory was married to David in spite of the previous contract. The Prince showed his preference for Lady Elizabeth by neglect of his bride, and a wild, vicious career cut short by his murder in Falkland Castle; and the Earl of March formed an affiance with the Percys of Northumberland, and under their banner became a bitter enemy to his native country. He eventually obtained a pardon, and the restoration of his estates, when the King's brother, the Duke of Albany, who was supposed to have been accessory to the murder of Prince David, acted as Regent during the detention in England of his nephew, the young King James I. But in 1440 the son of the Earl of March was deprived by an Act of the Scottish Parliament of all the lands he held in Dumfriesshire as a tenant of the Crown, although his brother John was created Earl of Murray, having married Lady Marjory Stewart, eldest daughter of King Robert II., and therefore aunt to James I. Her two grandsons, Thomas and James, went as hostages to England for the King's ransom in 1424.

This James Dunbar, who became Earl of Murray, and married Lady Janet Gordon, obtained the reversion of some of his great uncle's confiscated estates on the borders of Dumfriesshire, and, leaving only two daughters, his lands in Kirkpatrick went to the eldest, Lady Janet, married to James, second Lord Crichton, while his title and other estates went to his second daughter Mary, who married Archibald Douglas. She lost both the title and estates by her husband's participation in his brother's rebellion, which James, Earl of Douglas, inaugurated to revenge the assassination already mentioned of another brother by the King, James II., after supper in Stirling Castle. The Earl was joined by his relatives, as well as by the Earls of Murray and Ormond, and Lord Hamilton, and other chiefs; and, first proclaiming the cause of his disloyalty in the market place at Stirling, supported by 600 armed men, he proceeded to sack the town and burn it. The King was at Perth, but returned nearer to the scene of action, where in spite of a defeat they had sustained at Brechin Muir in 1452 the rebels still increased in power; and when the Parliament was sitting at Edinburgh to deprive them of their titles and estates, a letter was fastened in the night, to the door of the Parliament House, sealed by Douglas, Ormond, and Hamilton, renouncing all allegiance to the King. The chronicler of Auchinleck rites—"This Parliament was continued for fifteen days, and charged all manner of men to be at Edinburgh both foot and horse, each man for himself, both in burgh and land, under pain of death, and loss of their lands. The King himself passed on southwards with the host to Peebles, Selkirk, Dumfries, and other parts, and did no good, but destroyed the country right felonly, both of men, money, and victuals."

The Douglas rebellion was crushed at last by the battle of Langholm or Arkenholm, in Eskdale, on May 1, 1455, in which the insurgent lords were defeated by Maxwell, Johnstone, Scot, and Carlile. The Earl of Murray was killed, Ormond taken prisoner, and the lordship of Annandale and March, which

Douglas had possessed, was conferred on the King's second son, Alexander Duke of Albany (brother to James III.), a child of three years old. Before he was seven his father was killed by the bursting of a gun at the siege of Roxburgh, and twenty-four years afterwards he recalled Douglas from a long and weary exile in England to assist him in driving James III. from the throne. Henry VII. of England lent his aid to the unnatural brother, and an English army, accompanied by Douglas and Albany, entered Dumfriesshire, but they were defeated near Lochmaben by the combined forces of Maxwell, Johnstone, Cuthbert Murray of Cockpool, Crichton of Sanquhar, Carruthers of Holmains, and Charteris of Amisfield. Douglas was captured by an old vassal, Kirkpatrick of Ros. The King, in consideration of his age, spared his life, but consigned him to a monastery, and Albany's estates (the confiscated domains of the Earls of Murray and March on the borders) were appropriated to the Crown and redistributed, their late owner ending his days as an exile in France.

This Duke of Albany and his son, who bore the same title in the next century, carried to Paris several Scottish charters and other documents, which have never been restored. They are still preserved in the Hotel des Archives amongst those relating to Scotland, but also connected with France. In 1423 a letter from "Archambault, Earl of Douglas, Lord of Galloway, of Anaterdalle (Annandale), and Warden of the frontier of Scotland," engages that he will observe faithfully the old treaties existing between France and Scotland, and that he will come the following December, with several lords and men-at-arms and archers, to serve the King of France. In 1499 letters of naturalisation were given to Robert Jonston, a Scotsman in the service of the Queen of France, and in September, 1513, Louis XII., "considering the great service rendered to France by Scotland, principally against England, exempts for the future the Scots residing in France from the obligation to ask particularly letters of naturalisation," granting them *en masse* the right to make wills, to succeed as heirs, and to hold benefices as if they were Frenchmen.

The Scottish Archers, like the ancient Varangian Guard at Constantinople, were the defence on which the French kings most relied, and they seem from the names preserved to have been chiefly recruited from Dumfriesshire. The Archer Guard even stood round the choir when the French King was in church. In their credentials they were reminded of Abner and the various heroes of the Old Testament. In the reign of Louis XII., Count d'Irvin was their commander, and the force comprised 200 men. After the Union of England and Scotland, Scotsmen were no longer desired for this special duty, and the Swiss Guard, which was so much distinguished in the time of Louis XVI., supplied their place.

The Crichtons, who had promoted the disaffection of the Douglases, *[Douglas pointed out to a French ally how little advantage the English could obtain by a march into Scotland. "The houses of the gentlemen are small towers, with thick walls, which even fire will not destroy. As for the common people, they dwell in mere huts, and if the English choose to burn them, a few trees from the wood is only required to rebuild them."]* were enriched for their zeal on the side of the King's troops. According to Holinshed, the first Crichton came over from Hungary with Agatha, the widow of the Saxon Prince Edward, when her daughter married Malcolm III. in 1067. Thurstanus de Crichton was a witness to the foundation charter of the Abbey of Holyrood House in 1128, and Thomas de Crichton swore fealty to Edward I. for lands in Midlothian in 1296. His two sons founded the families of Sanquhar (now represented in the female line by the Marquis of Bute, who is also Earl of Dumfries) and of Frendraught. The eldest son became possessed of half the barony of Sanquhar through his wife, Isabelle de Ros, and subsequently purchased the whole, and his descendants married with the Murrays of Cockpool, and were mixed up in Annandale affairs. Sir Robert, afterwards Lord Crichton of Sanquhar, was made Coroner of Nithsdale in 1468, and he received from James III. a grant of the confiscated Douglas lands. His cousin, Sir William Crichton, the Chancellor, was also created Lord Crichton, and by the marriage of his eldest son, James, with Lady Janet Dunbar, the family succeeded to the barony of Frendraught-Gawin, the second son of Lord Crichton and Lady Janet, seems to have married a daughter or granddaughter of Johnstone of Elphinstone, as he received with his wife in 1479 the lands of Drumgrey, viz., Moling, Monyge, Rahills, &c., in the barony of Kirkmichael, which had been conferred by David II. on a former Adam Johnstone, and were afterwards confirmed to Sir Gilbert Johnstone of Elphinstone by Crown Charter in 1471. Margaret, the daughter of the second Lord Crichton of Sanquhar and his wife, Elizabeth Murray, married William Johnstone of Graitney, and was the ancestress of the Johnstones of Galabank and Fulford Hall. The Crichtons possessed lands in Dryfesdale, in Kirk-patrick, in the barony of Kirkmichael, and in the barony of Crawsfordtoun, now known as the parish of Crawford in Lanarkshire; but estates were increased or diminished with every generation at that period, from the custom of portioning off daughters and younger sons with land, for entails were not restricted to the senior male heir,

Sanquhar Castle

but to heirs male generally, or to both heirs, male and female; and this led to frequent exchanges between the head of a family and his cadets for the sake of concentrating his property. Hence, land that was brought by an heiress to a younger son is sometimes found a few years later in the hands of his elder brother's children, though he may himself have left heirs. An arrangement of this nature was made by the two families of Crichton.

Before the Reformation the Rectory of Sanquhar was leased from the Abbey of Holywood for £20 a year by the Crichtons. In 1494 Ninian Crichton, a layman, was parson of Sanquhar. He was tutor or guardian to his nephews and niece, the children of the second Baron Crichton, as appears by various decrees of the Lords in Council, in which a young Robert Lord Crichton is mentioned in 1525, who does not appear in any of the published pedigrees of the Crichton family, so he probably died before he came of age. His brother William, who succeeded him, married a daughter of Malcolm, Lord Fleming. Their grandson, Robert Crichton, was outlawed for having caused a fencing master to be murdered, and a description of his appearance was sent to Carlisle and Dumfries for his arrest. He is described as wearing a glass eye. He had lost his eye by accident when fencing some years before, and at the Court of France was asked by the King, Henry II., how it had happened. On being informed, Henry said—"And does the fellow live?" which Crichton interpreted as a reproach to himself, and forthwith gave orders to have the fencing-master killed. His heir [This William Lord Crichton is described in his retour as a natural son, one of the instances in which that term is used in Scottish records for a legitimate son. "Willielmus Crichton fillus naturalis Roberti Dominus Crichtoun de Sanquhar, haeres talliae dieti Roberti Dominus Crichtoun de Sanguhar patris in terries, &c."] ruined himself in 1617 by the splendid entertainment which he gave to James VI., who owed him a large sum of money, the proof of which he rolled up into a torch and lighted the King to bed with it. His estates had to be sold about thirteen years afterwards. The Crichtons and Douglases of Drumlanrig were prominent in promoting the second Reformation; but Crichton, the first Earl of Dumfries and Stair, was a supporter of the scheme for restoring the tithes to the church in the reign of Charles I.

Chapter Four

When the Castle of Alnwick was besieged by the Scots in 1093, the English garrison capitulated on condition that their King, Malcolm III., should in person receive the keys of the gates. They were brought on the top of a spear by Mowbray, a knight who purposely sent the point through the King's eye, causing his death. One of the King's companions was Ewen de Maccuswell, who married a daughter of the Lord of Galloway, with whom he received the Castle of Caerlaverock. It was in this stronghold that Edward Baliol – who resigned during the minority and exile of the son of Robert Bruce – took up his abode to make his last stand in Dumfriesshire, when the young David II. was restored to his father's throne. An English army had crossed the ford at the Solway to Baliol's assistance in 1332; but Caerlaverock was captured by Roger Kirkpatrick and John Stewart, in the name of King David, whose rival was compelled to retreat to England with a remnant of his foreign allies more anxious to carry off their plunder than to assist a losing cause. The Maxwells supported the Crown against Douglas in 1425, for he had hung their near relation, Lord Herries of Terregles. They married with the Carlyles, Murrays, Johnstones, and other Annandale families, and increased much in importance during the fifteenth and sixteenth centuries. In 1424, Sir Herbert Maxwell was made a Lord of Parliament by the title of Lord Maxwell of Caerlaverock, and a little later his family shared in the plunder of the Douglases, which brought them into Annandale, and they supplanted the Crichtons in Nithsdale. Lord Maxwell was imprisoned with Archibald Earl of Douglas, the Earl of Angus, Dunbar, Earl of March, and Hepburn of Hailes, when Murdoch, Duke of Albany, and his sons were seized by James I., and Murdoch was shut up in the Castle of Caerlaverock, but as it was not politic to kill the leaders of the independent Borderers, who might be used again by the English against Scotland, these chiefs were released after Murdoch's execution. Early in the 16th century, the Maxwells almost monopolised the Wardenship of the Borders, which up to that time they had held alternately with the Earls of March, the Earls of Douglas, the Johnstones, and the Murrays of Cockpool, and this produced much of the ill-feeling which existed between the Maxwells and the Johnstones for nearly 100 years.

The lord of Johnstone, who fought at Chevy Chase, had been a surety for the peace with England, in conjunction with Sir John Carlyle and Stuart of Castlemilk. His son Adam was distinguished in a battle fought against the English near Graitney or Gretna, where the Maxwells and

Sweetheart Abbey

Johnstones were opposed to the Welsh, the fiercest battalions of the enemy (1448). The contemporary chronicler of Auchinleck, writing from the victor's side, gives this brief description:—

"The 23d day of October was the battle of Lochmaben Stone, within the parish of St. Patrick, where Hugh of Douglas, Earl of Ormonde, was chieftain on the Scottish side, and with him Sir John Wallace of Cragy, the Lord of Johnstone, the Lord Somerville's son and heir, David Stewart of Castle Mylk, the Sheriff of Ayr, with other sundry gentles of the West land, and their men was called 4000. And on the English side the younger Percy and Sir John of Pennyton were chieftains, and with them 6000 of Englishmen; of whom their chieftains were taken and 1500 with them slain; drowned, 500."

The English chronicler Holinshed, writing in 1577, gives a more detailed account of the battle, and a larger number of slain. He also mentions Maxwell, whom the Scottish chronicler omits, although he was Warden of the Marches. His daughter was married to Sir Adam Johnstone's eldest son John. Sir Adam had married Lady Janet Dunbar, the youngest daughter of the rebel Earl of March. He had three sons besides his heir—Gilbert, who married Agnes, the heiress of Elphinstone, and was knighted for his services against the English; William, who died in 1468; and a Dumfries record mentions another son, James, as living in 1476. To judge by the legal cases in which Sir Gilbert Johnstone of Elphinstone and his son Adam were summoned by Dumfriesshire men, he lived chiefly in his native county till 1491, and then his name disappears; but most of his descendants migrated to Elphinstone, in Haddington, where they are now considered to be extinct. In 1484 Sir Gilbert Johnstone, as Sheriff of Edinburgh, opened the session of Parliament, and was also a guarantor of the Treaty of Peace with the English.

When the Albany and Douglas rebellion of 1483 was in progress, Sir Gilbert Johnstone, by order of James III., deputed his nephew Adam of Johnstone to arrest Sir James Liddell of Halkerstone and others of the insurgents. William and Robert of Johnstone witness Adam of Johnstone's formal summons to Sir James to surrender himself to the authorities. As stated, the rebels were finally crushed by the Dumfriesshire chiefs, among whom was Sir Gilbert's brother, the Lord of Johnstone.

Although some of the Carruthers family were faithful to the King, the Laird of Mouswald, their head, seems to have leagued with the Douglases. He was keeper of Lochmaben Castle, and the Auchinleck chronicler relates that in 1454 "the Lord of Johnstone's two sons took the Castle of Lochmaben from the Lord of Mouswald, called Carruthers, and his two sons, and all through treason of the porter; and since, the King gave them the keeping of the house to his profit." The King's adherents in Dumfriesshire—the Johnstones, Maxwells, Carruthers of Holmains, Crichton of Sanquhar, Cuthbert Murray of Cockpool, and Charteris of Amisfield—were rewarded with part of the confiscated estates of the Corries and Douglases, though it entailed long disputes with the relatives of the ancient possessors. In 1516, we find James Johnstone of that ilk confrmed by a Royal Charter in the barony of Corrie, which had been held in the previous century by the Corrie family in conjunction with Newbie, Stapleton, and the parish of St. Patrick, now divided into Kirkpatrick-Fleming and Gretna, and which the Corries had obtained from the Carliles, while in 1494 John Murray had been returned heir to his father Cuthbert in the hereditary lands of Cockpool, Ryvel or Ruthwell, as well as of Rampatrick, or Redkirk, also part of the Corrie property.

As the question whether Newbie Castle and Gretna or Graitney passed direct from the Corries to the Lord of Johnstone has been one of dispute, not only when the Annandale peerage claims were last tried, but in 1772, in a case heard before the Scottish Courts, when the Earl of Hopetoun, curator-in-law of the last Marquis of Annandale, produced on his behalf the charter settling Newbie on William Johnstone of Gretna, and his wife, Margaret Crichton, in 1541, we may here make some allusion to this subject. The Counsel for the Marquis, who was trying to prove his right to certain fisheries from remote times, held that the manner in which Newbie afterwards passed to the Lord of Johnstone in 1607 shewed that William Johnstone's descendants were cadets of his house. Chalmers, in his Biographia, and the compiler of the "New Statistical History of Scotland," were impressed with this notion. The last states that many Johnstones of Annandale are interred under the old church at Gretna; and these Johnstones were all William's descendants. The author of the "Biography of Eminent Scotsmen" took the same view, and also the editor of the New Monthly Review in his obituary of the representative of William's family in 1802. So did the second Marquis when he put Johnstone of Gretna in his entail. The Johnstones of Gretna are described in the oldest peerages (Crawford of 1716, and Nesbitt, published by Royal authority in 1722) as cadets of Johnstone of that Ilk; and in various local histories the Johnstones of Gretna and Newbie are also described as his cadets. The same claim is engraved on the monument of John Johnstone of Galabank, their descendant in 1774, when the last Marquis was alive, and his mother and two half brothers resided at Comlongon Castle, in the immediate neighbourhood, and its authority was not called in question. The connection was, therefore, supported by common repute.

But now to proved facts. In 1453 a Gilbert de Johnstone de Gretna signed a retour at Dumfries for Lord Maxwell, whose sister was married to the eldest son of Sir Adam Johnstone. Sir Adam's father was named Gilbert, and his second son was named Gilbert, and was able to write, not a common accomplishment at that time. Sir Adam was then Warden of the Borders, and would therefore be likely to put a near relative into Gretna, as it was the gateway to England, and commanded his own neighbouring estates at Cavertsholme and Dunskellie. Retours were signed by relations and connections, and as no mere tenant in a distant place would have been called upon to sign Lord Maxwell's retour at Dumfries when he had connections much nearer, it is probable that Gilbert Johnstone of Gretna was Gilbert, the second son of Sir Adam, or else a brother of Sir Adam, and that he was custodian of Gretna Tower, a Border fortress, when his relative was Warden. Unless the Annan was navigable higher up than it is now, it is difficult to see how the lairds of Johnstone could have been "naval admirals," have owned "ships to trade with English ports," or, considering the small extent of the family estates inland, could have carried sufficient weight on the borders to act as Constables and Wardens, a hundred and fifty years earlier, if they had no footing on the Solway; and Graitney Tower and Saltcoats, with a few maritime villages afterwards owned by William Johnstone of Graitney and Newbie, are the only points not claimed elsewhere. Hoddam was then owned by the piratical Lord Herries of Terregles. During the rest of the 15th century, there is no mention of Gretna in

31

any record; but a Thomas Johnstone, described as of Gartno—that is, Gret-na—is alluded to in a justiciary case of 1504. He was not a judge of the assize. There is no sasine concerning him in existence, and nothing to show that he was a landowner or had any connection with William Johnstone, the young lord of Gartno, who appears in 1513.

In 1511 an Adam Johnstone de Newbie appears as a judge of the assize at Edinburgh. Adam of Johnstone of that Ilk was dead in 1509, when his son James was returned his heir. His family, of all the leaders of the King's party against the Douglas rebellion, would have had no share in the spoil if he had not been rewarded with some of the lands of the rebel Corries, who, as before stated, owned the baronies of Corrie and of Newbie, Mylnfleld, Robgill, Cum-mertrees, Bonshaw, and Stapleton, within a mile of Gretna, and adjoining the Laird of Johnstone's property at Dunskellie, Cavertsholme, and Kirkpatrick-Fleming. They would naturally prefer the estates which intersected their own lands, and being good soldiers and nearly related, as well as friends at that time with the Warden of the Borders, he would have been likely to approve of their infeftment into the part of the forfeited demesne, which bordered on England, to aid him in the defence of the country. In 1508-9 the Lord of John-stone and Adam Johnstone were two of the judges of assize who convicted William Carruthers of uplifting cattle from the lands of Newbie. This Lord of Johnstone was Adam, who died a month or two later. The other Adam John-stone on the assize was probably the same as Adam Johnstone of Newbie mentioned in 1511, and may have been the second son of the Laird, or his grandson, afterwards known as Adam Johnstone of Corrie.

In 1516 James Johnstone of that Ilk obtained a charter confirming him in the possession of the Barony of Corrie. He had previously received a charter of the Barony of Johnstone, the advowson of the Church of Johnstone, the lands of Wamphray, the mill and lands at Dunskellie, in Kirkpatrick-Fleming, and the lands of Cavertsholme (near Gretna) owned by his father, "which lands," it states, "were sequestrated at the King's instance for certain fines of Justice Courts, which now his Majesty freely discharges, and dispones the land to him again." This sequestration must have taken place after James IV. visited Dumfries in August 1504, and held an assize, in person, as on that occasion Adam Johnstone was pledge for his eldest son, James. While the Lord of John-stone was ejected from the Barony of Johnstone and his residence at Dunskel-lie he would be likely to live at Graitney with his immediate followers. The Justiciary Records are not always very exact in their descriptions, as James Johnstone is described as the Laird of Johnstone in his father's lifetime. He was for some years an outlaw, but in 1513 he acted as pledge at Dumfries for his relative, Adam Scot, and for several Johnstones, including William, the young lord of Gartno (Gretna or Graitney), and a "David Johnstone, brother to John Johnstone in Bartycupen," which was not far from Lochwood, and he was fined for their non-appearance. A man began life early at that date, and as Robert Johnstone of Racleuch was only eleven years old when we find his name among those respited in 1594 for arson and slaughter, William of Gretna may have been no older in 1513. The David and John mentioned were probably James Johnstone's two illegitimate sons of that name. Gretna was not a lairdship, and those described as of Gretna could not have been landowners, while William being distinguished by the term "young laird," shows he was the son of a laird, and he could not have made the good marriage he did if he had been a mere tenant. In the affair for which he was summoned in 1513, a relative of Lord Crichton, the Sheriff, had been killed in an attack on Dumfries by Maxwell and his followers, including these Johnstones, while the assize was being held. Not only did the Laird of Johnstone protect William and David, but he offered to pay half the sum adjudged by the Lords in Council (See Acta Dom. Con. 25, f. 168, t. 172, 1513) to be paid by Lord Maxwell to the injured party, Lord Crichton. [In most instances the Constables of the Borders were given lands on condition that they maintained garrisons, and kept lighted beacons on the towers near the English frontier. Hoddam and Graitney were very important ones. Graitney is a little to the east of the village.]

James, Laird of Johnstone, died in August, 1524. On October 14, 1527, we find an entry in the Justiciary Records that John Johnstone of that Ilk, John, Andrew, and Roland Bell, William and Matthew Johnstone, were charged with the cruel murder of Symon Armstrong, James Douglas of Drumlanrig being their cautioner; and failing to appear, they were all denounced rebels, which, with a subsequent sequestration, accounts for the Johnstone estates being in ward four years. John Johnstone entailed his lands in 1542, and mentions four brothers: Adam of Corrie, William, Symon, and John. There were also two illegitimate brothers, David and John, so that in one family there were three brothers named John. Adam, the second brother, had inherited the barony of Corrie, and it seems likely that he was the Adam Johnstone of Newbie mentioned in 1511, and had later received from his father the more secure possessions of Corrie. The Corrie family continued to claim Newbie, and to style themselves of Newbie, as late as 1630, but Thomas Corrie was an outlaw some time before 1523, and being respited in 1527, he instituted proceedings against William Johnstone of Graitney, who for three years past (i.e., since the death of the laird of Johnstone) had occupied the lands of Newbie. Newbie was worth only six pounds a year less than the Barony of Johnstone, and, as we have stated, with its dependencies intersected the estate of Johnstone of that Ilk, and was a near neighbour to his chief residence, Dunskellie. It is clear that William Johnstone could not have taken possession of so large an estate without the concurrence of the great Annandale chief; and Gretna, it appears from later documents, was only held in feu from the Murrays of Cockpool. The mistake of calling a man laird of a place when he lived there, but was only son or brother of a laird, occurs in the Acta Dom. Con. in 1594 with regard to a Johnstone of Newbie. At last William Johnstone purchased a clear right to Newbie from Thomas Corrie, who was to retain a life interest in it, but was killed at the battle of Pinkie in 1547.

In 1541 William Johnstone obtained a charter, which the late Sir John Holker, Attorney-General, described as the most extraordinary which had ever been brought before the House of Lords. He entailed Newbie and its lands,--but not Gretna—first, on his own and his wife's (Margaret Crichton) legitimate children; secondly, on his own legitimate male heirs; thirdly, on his son George and his heirs; fourthly, on his brother David and his heirs; fifthly, on his son Herbert and his heirs; sixthly, on his son John and his heirs; seventhly, on his brother John and his heirs. These brothers and sons mentioned by name were undoubtedly illegitimate, and the fact that the Laird of Johnstone and his brother William had at the same period two illegitimate brothers, named David and John, seemed, with the evidence already given, to point to the conclusion that they were the same people, and that William Johnstone of Graitney and Newbie was identical with William, the second brother of the laird. Also, the fact that Graitney descended to William's illegitimate son George, while Newbie went to his eldest legitimate son John, who in 1565 was returned his father's nearest and legitimate heir, would further show that Graitney was not regarded as a special hereditary possession of his family. This John, second Baron of Newbie, is the ancestor of the Johnstones of Galabank and now of Fulford Hall. It appeared as if James, lord of Johnstone, had bequeathed the confiscated Corrie property to his second and third sons, the elder receiving Corrie, for which he had obtained a regular charter; the other Newbie, for which he had to enforce his claim. Another brother, James of Wamphray, is not mentioned in the entail, but in 1550 he formed a bond of manrent with the laird. The descendants of George Johnstone of Graitney died out in the male line, and their present representative in the female line is Lord Ruthven. In 1592, they bore the arms of Johnstone of that Ilk, charged with two mullets to show cadency, and a different crest to denote legitimized bastardy. We learn by the charters of 1536 and 1541 concerning William of Graitney that he bore the same arms as Johnstone of that Ilk, proving that he was legitimate.

In 1546 the English invaded Scotland, and razed Annan to the ground, whereupon the neighbouring chiefs gave in their submission, and swore fidelity to the English King. Holinshed's "Scottish History," published in 1577, mentions the Laird of Newbie among them, but no other representative of the Johnstones; while the English State papers describe William, the brother of the Laird, as surrendering on behalf of the Johnstones. They also speak of George Johnstone (William of Newbie and Graitney eldest illegitimate son) as heading the Newbie dependants. The Laird of Johnstone was a prisoner, and his next brother (Adam) dead; but his nephew, James of Corrie, a man of full age, was also a prisoner among the English. In 1548 an Act of the Scottish Parliament outlawed the Laird of Newbie and several other chiefs, but no other representative of Johnstone of that Ilk, for their surrender, and from this period William Johnstone of Newbie disappears. In 1558 William Johnstone, brother-german to the laird, signs (with his hand at the pen) a renunciation of his rights to Hartope, in Nithsdale, and as these lands were part of the Crichton property, the fact of William Johnstone, Laird of' Newbie,, being married to a Crichton seemed another proof of the identity of these Williams, particularly as at that period the English occupied Newbie and Gretna, and he had been outlawed as Laird of Newbie, so would hardly have signed his name with that appellation. In 1542, when the Johnstone property was provisionally entailed on the Laird's brother William, he is simply mentioned as brother-german to the Laird, but he did not possess the life-rent of Newbie till 1557, and seems to have had no real property in Gretna till 1544 (in which year William, brother of the Laird, signed his name himself as witness to Simon Carruthers, *[Married to Marion Johnstone]* his brother-in-law), and when, by letters under the Privy Seal, a grant of the non-entres of Gretna, that had been held by the Crown since the decease of "the late Johnstone, his father," is made to William of Gretna until such time as another heir should appear. The son and heir of this William in 1569 acted as pledge for the Laird of Johnstone and his clan, thereby preserving the castles of his chief from being destroyed by the Regent Murray after the outbreak on behalf of Queen Mary. He was a guardian of the peace with the English, and was one of the kinsmen selected by the Laird of Johnstone to adjust his quarrel with Lord Maxwell in 1574. His son, Edward Johnstone, was curator to the young Laird of Johnstone in 1608, and had possession of the Annandale charter chest, which still contains many charters concerning the Newbie family. In 1613 a Crown charter states that all the old papers concerning Gretna had been destroyed in the wars and conflagrations of which it had been the centre, so it appears as if William Johnstone had been the custodian of the fortified tower at Gretna—an important post before the Union of the Crowns. His wife's mother, Elizabeth, was the daughter of Cuthbert Murray of Cockpool. Margaret Crichton's father was Sir Robert Crichton, Lord of Sanquhar, dead before 1517, when Ninian Crichton is mentioned as her guardian; and James and Ninian Crichton were cautioners for William Johnstone in 1535, with regard to the contract with the Corries of Newbie.

But the point which weighed against the claim of the descendants of William Johnstone of Gretna and Newbie, that their ancestor was identical with the third son of the Laird of Johnstone, was the discovery of a precept for a charter under the Privy Seal of 1543. It had been overlooked by two searchers in the Register House at Edinburgh, but a copy was found among the papers of a deceased advocate, which brought it to light. It was a precept of legitimation for George, Herbert, and John, the illegitimate sons of William Johnstone of Gretna, and of his illegitimate brother John, the natural son of the late William Johnstone of Gretna—this last name of the late William, &c., being added over the line, as if an afterthought on the part of the clerk. Twenty pounds had been paid for this precept, which was not signed or followed by any charter, so could never have been carried out, as a precept of legitimation requires to be confirmed by three charters to be effective; and. it was written in such bad Latin that it might have been construed that one William was the brother of the other, and that John was the natural son of the deceased one. Just a month after the date of this precept there was another precept for a charter to legitimatise David and John, the natural sons of James, the Laird of Johnstone of that Ilk, and this precept was given gratis, and followed by a charter. It might have been suggested that the first was erroneous, and did not include William's illegitimate brother David, and that the second, which was issued just sufficiently long after to allow of a journey from Edinburgh to Annan and back again, was a correction of the first, and hence given without a fee; that William Johnstone of Newbie had desired the legitimation of the two brothers whom he had named in his entail, not of his sons, who might in that case have interfered with the rights of his and Margaret Crichton's legitimate son John; and that the father's name--the late William Johnstone of Gretna—had been ignorantly added by the clerk, as it was usual in such cases to give the father's name, and "William Johnstone, young Lord of Gartno," [Most family histories conjecture that the marriage of Lady Janet Dunbar with Sir Adam Johnstone took place only in 1448; but that is not likely (and there is no proof that he had a previous wife), if she were the mother, as is alleged, of his younger son Sir Gilbert Johnstone of Elphinstone, for her grandson (by her first husband, Sir John Seton) was in possession of his grandfather's estates in 1441, and in 1448 he was Ambassador Extraordinary to the Court of England. Her eldest son, the father of this grandson, was killed in battle in 1424, and her father was a Commissioner of the Peace with England in 1380. Her eldest sister had been betrothed to David, Prince of Scotland, an engagement broken off before 1402.] was a name found in the Justiciary Records in Edinburgh, as sharing in an affray in 1513. But even if the two Williams were not identical they were evidently closely related.

Sir Frederick Johnstone of Westerhall claimed the Annandale Peerages on the ground that his ancestor Matthew was a son of Sir Adam Johnstone, who died in 1455. Sir Adam left four sons—John, his heir; Gilbert of Elphinstone; [Mr Archibald Johnstone of Herriothill, Edinburgh, writes that he believes himself to be a descendant of the Johnstones of Elphinstone (whom two lawsuits have declared to be extinct in the male line). They exported coal from Haddington till it was stopped by an order from the Lords in Council, who feared the supply would become exhausted. The home trade was overstocked, and having to support all the work people without remuneration they were obliged to dispose of their lands, and removed to Newmonkland, where they again farmed and mined for coal about 1693. But the heiresses of Elphinstone, as of Wamphray, in more than one instance married Johnstones of another branch, in accordance with their father's will, and in this way their maiden name remained to their descendants.] William, who died 1468; James, who was living in 1476; and an old peerage includes Adam of Pensakke, who was dead, but leaving a son Robert before 1495. Unlike the Johnstones of Galabank and Fulford Hall, Sir Frederick was descended almost invariably from eldest sons. Matthew is described as armiger or esquire in 1455. There are several Matthew Johnstones on record in that century, but it is a name absent from the direct line of Johnstones of that Ilk. Sir Frederick's ancestor received lands in Lanarkshire for service against the rebel Douglas; and his descendants were from that time little seen in Dumfriesshire till the close of the 16th century, when they sold their property in Lanarkshire, and came to live on their present demesne, the head of their house having married the sister of Johnstone of that Ilk. They have long been reported to be an early branch of the Johnstones of Lochwood, but they were unable to produce proof of the connection of the two families at any special link. Their claim, like that of Mr Edward Johnstone of Fulford Hall, was therefore declared to be not proved to the satisfaction of the House of Lords in 1881.

Chapter Five

The Grahames, including the Duke of Montrose, and the Grahams of Mossknowe, [Sir R. Graham of Esk, born 1843, and the Grahames of Netherby represent the English branch. Colonel Graham of Mossknowe, born 1797, had William (born 1832), John Gordon, Charles Stewart, Rosina, Grace (married Captain Murray, R.M.), and Clementina.] and the other parts of Dumfriesshire, claim descent from King Grime, a Scottish sovereign who reigned for a short time in 1010. Some of the family were more English than Scotch, for they generally joined the enemy when Scotland was invaded, and if pursued for a theft retreated into Cumberland, and claimed protection as Englishmen. Not long before the Union of the two crowns their depredations in both countries nearly caused a war. The Laird of Johnstone was deputed to keep them in order; and at last, after 1603, James VI. exiled the greater part of them to Ireland with the strictest orders never to return, "because," as he said in his proclamation, "they do all confess themselves to be no meet persons to live in these countries, and also to the intent that their lands may be inhabited by others of good and honest conversation." "The vulgar sort, as they are termed in the legal procedure, were always easily dealt with by execution, but it was the sons and brothers of the lairds who were the great obstacles to peace. Among Lord Muncaster's charters there are some curious details. "Richie Grahame," brother of the lord of Netherby, it was pointed out, was the great offender, and it would cause an outcry if others were banished and he allowed to remain. Some of his relations escaped into Scotland, where, we hear, they were protected by Johnstones, Carliles, and Irvings, "who are related to them." A Christopher Irving was hung with some of the murderers of Carmichael (the Scottish Warden). Simon de Musgrave, of a distinguished English border family, is described as one of this lawless crew, and among them a Herbert Johnstone was expelled, whose descendants still live in Ireland. Lord Cumberland helped to pay the expense of their transportation in return for a gift of their land.

In the reign of Charles I. Sir Richard Grahame of Netherby obtained an alteration of the boundary line between England and Scotland, so that his property in the parish of Kirkandrews-upon-Esk might in future be English ground. He had accompanied Charles, when Prince of Wales, on a journey through France and Spain; and Wotton relates the following anecdote:—

"They were entered into the deep time of Lent, and could get no flesh in their inns. There was near Bayonne a herd of goats, with their young ones; upon the sight whereof Sir Richard Grahame tells the Marquis of Buckingham that he would snap one of the kids, and make some shift to carry him snug to their lodging. Which the Prince overhearing, "Why, Richard," says he, "do you think you may practise here your old tricks upon the Borders?" Upon which words they, in the first place, gave the goat herd good contentment; and then while the Marquis and Richard, being both on foot, were chasing the kid about the stock, the Prince from horseback killed him in the head with a pistol." The Grahames are enumerated among the followers of Douglas at Otterbourne in 1387—

He chose the Gordons and the Graemes,
With them the Lindsays light and gay;
But the Jardines will not with him ride,
And they rue it to this day.

The name of Gordon is the same as that of Bertrand de Jourdain, the French archer who shot Richard I. at Chalons in 1199. It is found in Scotland about that period, and Sir Adam Gordon, in 1297, [Represented by David Gordon, Esq. of Culvennan, Kirkcudbright-shire, born 1828, and by Sir William Gordon of Earlston, born 1830.] was a faithful adherent to Sir William Wallace. His descendants married with the Crichtons and Murrays, and owned lands in Dumfriesshire, where they became renowned as the Lords of Lochinvar. The title of Viscount Kenmure was conferred on Sir John Gordon by Charles I. in 1633. His last direct descendant, the Hon. Louisa Bellamy Gordon, sister and heiress of Adam, 11th Viscount Kenmure, and widow of Charles Bellamy, died May 31, 1886.

The Jardines of Applegirth are descendants of Jardin or Gardin, who came over with the Conqueror, and their signatures are attached to charters a century after this date. They inter-married with the first families in Dumfriesshire, and appear as Knights in the 14th century, when Spedlings Castle in Lochmaben was their possession. Their baronetcy dates from 1672. The late Sir William Jardine of Applegirth was much distinguished for his scientific attainments.

The Kirkpatricks are a Celtic family found very early in Scottish history, and like the Jardines have required no higher title than "chevalier" to give lustre to an ancient name. Closeburn [The Castle contained an oubliette or secret dungeon. It passed from the Kirkpatricks more than a 100 years ago.] was granted to Ivon Kirkpatrick in 1232, by Alexander II. of Scotland, and the great-grandson of this Ivon was the Knight who stabbed the dying Cumyn at the back of the High Altar in the Grey Friars Church in Dumfries in 1305. Cumyn and Robert Bruce had a dispute, and Bruce leaving the church in some agitation met Kirkpatrick, who asked him what had happened. "I doubt," said Bruce, "I have slain the Cumyn." "You doubt," cried Kirkpatrick, "I'se mak sicker" (I will make sure), an expression which his family afterwards adopted as their motto, and rushing in with Sir James Lindsay they despatched first Cumyn, and then his uncle, Sir Robert Cumyn, who was hurrying into the church. Duncan Kirkpatrick, the father of this assassin, had in 1280 married the daughter of Sir David Carlile of Torthorwald, who owned estates about Annan and Kirkpatrick-Fleming. He is mentioned in the following lines by Blind Harry, the minstrel:—

Kirkpatrick that cruel was and keyne,
In Esdaill wod that yer he had been;
With Englishmen he could noch weill accord;
Of Torthorwald he baron was and lord;
Of kyne he was to Wallace modyr ner.

The family of Cumyn are now represented by Sir William Gordon Cumming, fourth baronet, born in 1848. A Comin appears on the Roll of Battle Abbey, but Holinshed refers their origin to 1124. "In the days of this King Alexander, the kindred of the Cummings had their beginning by one John Cumming, a man of great prowess and valiancy, obtaining of the King in respect thereof certain small portions of land in Scotland."

One branch of the Kirkpatricks died out in Thomas Kirkpatrick of Auld-girth, about 1665, and his sister Janet married John Johnstone of Galabank in 1670. The present representative is Sir James Kirkpatrick, whose baronetcy dates from 1685. A scion of the family settled at Malaga early in the present century as agent to a Scottish wine merchant, and was very useful to the commissariat department of the British army in the Peninsular War. He had three daughters, whose brilliant complexion and fair hair, as well as handsome fortunes, were the admiration of the Spanish dons, and among frequent visitors at his house was the Count de Teba, an impoverished nobleman of ancient lineage, who had served under the French and been frightfully injured by an explosion, which, it is said, had deprived him of a leg and an arm. Yet, in course of time, the second of the Miss Kirkpatricks became first the Countess de Teba, and a little later, on her husband succeeding to a distant relative's title and estate, Countess de Montijo, better known as the mother of the ex-Empress of the French. Some difficulty was raised by the Spanish Court, on the ground that it was a mésalliance; but her father, who died insolvent, applied to the well known antiquary, Mr Kirkpatrick Sharpe, for the Kirkpatrick pedigree, and when it was handed over to the authorities who had a right to veto the marriage of a grandee it was considered sufficient proof of the lady's noble blood. Another sister married a wine grower in Andalusia, and the third, an official employed in the Commissariat of the British army. The Count de Teba and Montijo died in 1823, after being separated from his wife, as is shown by a lawsuit, a few years later.

The Flemings, supposed to descend from a native of Flanders, were in ancient times barons in the parish of St. Patrick, part of which preserves their name in its modern style, Kirkpatrick-Fleming. A branch of the family were created Earls of Wigton, but the title became extinct in 1747. It was assumed at that time by Charles Ross Fleming, M.D., of Dublin, eldest son of the Rev. James Fleming of Kilkenny, and he voted without challenge at Holyrood in several elections of Scottish representative Peers. In 1761 he was ordered to appear before the House of Lords and show by what authority he took that title, whereupon he presented a petition in the usual form, praying their Lordships to allow him to take up the honours, dignities, &c.; but it was decided that he had not proved his claim. He died October 18, 1769, and seven years later his son, Hamilton Fleming, presented a petition to the House of Lords to the same effect, but was also unable to prove his descent to the satisfaction of the House. His only child, Harriet, married William Gyll, Esq. of Wyradisbury House, Bucks.

The Carruthers family appear to have been in Dumfriesshire as far back as the Kirkpatricks, and are first found on the lands of Carruthers in the modern parish of Middlebie. Thomas, son of Robert Carruthers, received a grant of Mouswald from Robert Bruce. Their estate stretched northward into the district of Wamphray, which they shared with the Laird of Johnstone, and they were made Barons of Mouswald in the 15th century. Simon Carruthers and his wife, Catherine Carlile, had a charter of lands in Cummertrees in 1516, and their son Simon married Agnes, a daughter of Murray of Cockpool. Their grandson, Simon, married Marion Johnstone, and left two daughters, Janet and Marion. The elder married Rorison of Barndennoch, and a curious bond relating to the younger daughter is dated Edinburgh, September 13, 1563— "The which day Thomas Borthick of Pryneade and Michael Borthick of Glengall became pledges and securities for Marion Carruthers, one of the two heiresses of Mouswald, that she shall not marry any chief traitor nor broken man (i. e., outlaw and adventurer not belonging to a clan) of the country, nor join herself with any such person under the pain of one thousand pounds."

In 1426 Roger Carruthers, a son of the Laird of Mouswald, had a charter from Douglas, Lord of Galloway and Annandale, of Holmains, with Dalton and other lands; and his descendants branched off into the families of Holmains, [John Carruthers of Holmains, married to Charlotte, daughter of Sir Robert Laurie of Maxwelton, was obliged to sell his family property in the last century in consequence of the series of calamities to which Dumfriesshire had been subjected, culminating in bank failures, spreading general ruin. His descendants died out in the male line, but the family is represented in the female by his great grandson, the Rev. William Mitchell Carruthers, eldest son of the late General St. Leger Mitchell, born 1853, incumbent of Brunswick Chapel, Mayfair; married, and has issue. In 1788, when the franchise was very limited, John Carruthers is described as having no longer a vote, and it is remarkable that all who were then stated in a secret memoir to have any fortune or sufficient estate to qualify them were in a profession or business, or had acquired wealth elsewhere than in Dumfriesshire. There were 52 voters, and persons were incapacitated who in the year preceding an election had been twice present at divine service where the officiating minister had not taken the oath to King George, nor prayed for the Royal family. Sir James Kirkpatrick was a lawyer; also Charles Share of Hoddom, who was keeper of the harriers to the Prince of Wales. Patrick Miller of Dalswinton had made his fortune as a banker at Glasgow, and Sir Robert Herries was a banker in London; Alexander Fergusson of Craigdarroch was an advocate; Dr James Hunter and his two brothers, one a minister and the other a Writer to the Signet; Sir William Pulteney, a barrister, and his young cousin, Richard Berup de Johnstone (ancestor to Lord Derwent), whose fortune was derived from his grandfather, a Dutch merchant; Maxwell of Barncleugh; the Baronet of Westerhall, described as a very independent honest man, his brothers; John Johnstone of Donovan, described as immensely rich; Hugh Corrie and Thomas Goldie, both writers; David Armstrong and William Copeland, advocates; William Elliot of Arkletoun; Sir Wm. Maxwell of Springkell; George Milligan Johnstone of Corhead and George Johnston of Cowhill, both merchants and new proprietors; Sir R. Grierson's brother was a merchant; Mackie of Palgowan, in the English Civil Service; Sir William Maxwell Springkell, Bart.; William Jardine: and Robert Wightman Henderson, conclude the list.] Wormanbie, [This branch became extinct in the male line with the late D.A. Carruthers, Esq., whose grandson, Louis Carruthers Salkeld, now owns the estate.] and Dormont. They owned estates bordering on Lockerbie, Lochmaben, Annan, and Kirkpatrick-Fleming; and when the town of Annan received a charter in 1538, they prevented the boundary of the burgh being defined where it joined their property, so that at some future time they might quietly annex it. The Laird of Holmains, with 162 followers, was compelled to surrender to the English after the battle of Pinkie, in 1547, and was among those chiefs who were declared traitors by the Parliament of Scotland in 1548. This Laird John Carruthers was married to Blanche Murray of Cockpool, and one of their daughters married Gilbert Johnstone of Wamphray. Another (Marion) married John Johnstone of Newbie A son of Carruthers was parson of Wamphray, which at that period was by no means the same as having taken holy orders; for one of the crimes against which John Knox preached most loudly was the alienation of the Church lands and tithes to secular purposes—a practice carried to an extreme in Scotland before the Reformation. Even the Abbots were sometimes seculars. [Some of the irregularities in Church matters were probably due to a foreign ecclesiastical government being established in the country. In the reign of Henry III. the Pope placed 400 Italians in English benefices and many foreign priests received preferment in Scotland before the Reformation. The services and religious books were in Latin, and although the Church lands were spared in the rules of ordinary warfare, this custom was not regarded in the English and Scottish wars. In many cases the vicars and monks were aliens, and looked upon by both armies with national dislike.] There is an agreement, dated January, 1561, between Robert Johnstone, himself a lay parson of Lochmaben, and Margaret M'Clellan, the widow of his uncle, James Johnstone of Wamphray, to the effect that, "Forasmuch as the said Robert having obtained a lease of Sir James Carruthers, parson of Wamphray, of the whole parsonage and vicarage, tithes, fruits, and endowments pertaining to the said parsonage and vicarage, for the space of his life-time, and the said Margaret having had the parsonage, vicarage, and endowments thereof from the said Sir James for his lifetime before the lease since made to the said Robert, which was wrongly and evil given against all law and good conscience, and in hurt and prejudice of the said Margaret's lease before expressed; therefore the said Robert gives up the letters of lease to the said Margaret to be used by her from, hence-forth." Signed by James Rigg, Mungo Carmichael, and the master of Maxwell. Margaret being unable to write her hand was guided by the notary.

Throughout the 15th, 16th, and 17th centuries the Carlyles appear in public transactions connected with the county of Dumfries. In 1435 Sir William Carlyle accompanied a body of 6000 archers to France, when the daughter of James I. was married to the Dauphin, afterwards Louis XI. in 1435. This knight was infefted in Brydekirk among other estates, before 1466. He gave a bell to the town of Dumfries, bearing the inscription in old Latin:—"William de Car-liel, Lord of Torthorwald, caused me to be made in honour of St. Michael, in the year of our Lord, 1443." His son Sir John was created Lord Carlyle of Tor-thorwald in 1471; and the second peer entered into a bond in 1496, that he and his spouse "should be harmless of William Carlile, his grandson and heir, who had married a daughter of Lord Maxwell, and that the said William should be harmless of Lord Carlile." John Johnstone of that Ilk (a brother or uncle to the laird, whose name was Adam) was the security. A similar bond was signed a month before by the same John Johnstone and his spouse, and Lord Carlyle, viz., that they should keep the peace. In 1573, Michael, Lord Car-lyle, having survived his eldest son, who left only a daughter, executed a deed bequeathing his title and estates to his second son. It is witnessed by Adam Carlyle of Brydekirk, his near relation, and by Alexander, son and heir of this Adam Carlyle; also, by John Carlyle of Brakenthwaite, Peter Carlyle, son of Lord Carlyle, and others. But after his death the inheritance was long disputed between his granddaughter Elizabeth and her uncle Michael, and eventually decided in favour of the lady, who married Sir James Douglas of Parkhead. After both had been almost ruined by the contest, the eldest son of Elizabeth and Sir James Douglas was recreated Lord Carlyle in 1609. The male descent of Michael, fourth Lord Carlyle, still claimed the ancient barony in 1764. Alex-ander Carlyle, Laird of Brydekirk, and his son Adam, the young laird, are men-tioned by Sir Thomas Carleton, the English Warden of the Borders in 1547, as the only gentry in Annandale, Liddesdale, and Nithsdale who had never sub-mitted to the English, except Douglas of Drumlanrig. His family branched off into several representatives. One of these, Adam Carlyle, was a merchant and bailie of Annan. He married Janet Muirhead, and left two children—James, whose descendants migrated to Paisley, and now live in England, and Isobel, married to Edward Johnstone of the family of Newbie and Galabank. He died in 1686, and lies buried under a legible inscription in the old churchyard in Annan, close to the grave of his daughter and her husband.

The Murrays of Cockpool descend from a knight who married the sister of Thomas Randolph, the first Earl of Murray, in the reign of Alexander III, and were established at Comlongon and Ryvel, or Ruthwell, in 1331. John Murray was returned heir to his father Cuthbert in the lands of Cockpool, Ryvel, and Redkirk, July 17, 1494. At the union of the two crowns a commission sat for twenty years to inquire into the titles of the landowners on the Borders, and to ensure their pacification; and as during the wars of which that district had constantly been the centre many title-deeds were destroyed in burnt houses and towns, it was a splendid opportunity for those in favour at Court to recover what they could prove had belonged to their families centuries before, if not to increase their possessions where they really had no claim. James Murray of Cockpool, a Royal favourite, and a gentleman of the Bedchamber, increased his property much during that twenty years, and his descendant in the female line, the present Earl of Mansfield, now owns Gretna, which Murray bought back from the Johnstones in 1618. His brother John received the titles of Viscount Annand and Earl of Annandale, which became extinct in 1658. James Murray, only son of this John, retired into England, and lived there privately during the Civil War. His widow married his distant relative, David Murray, lord of Scone, and Viscount Stormont, whose eldest son married Marjory, daughter of David Scot of Scotstarvit, and grand-daughter through female descents of James Murray of Cockpool. This marriage united the Murray's property in Dumfriesshire to the Perthshire estates of the Murrays of Scone and Stormont.

The Murrays of Scone had already produced one eminent Scottish lawyer, but the most celebrated of the family was the fourth son of David, sixth Viscount Stormont, and of Marjory Scot—William, created Earl of Mansfield, who was born at Comlongon Castle in 1742. He is immortalised by a statue in Westminster Abbey, and by the talents which raised him from an almost penniless younger son to be Solicitor-General, Attorney-General, Lord Chief Justice, and a member of the Cabinet. He married a daughter of the Earl of Winchelsea, and owing to the extinction of the lineage of his three elder brothers his descendant inherits the family title of Stormont as well as that of Mansfield.

The ford across the mouth of the Esk where it flows in the Solway was the favourite passage by which the English entered Scotland, and the Scots marched through it to assault Carlisle; so that the post of guard was conferred by the English King on a notably worthy warrior. The tract between the Esk and Sark, when Edward III was driven from Dumfriesshire, fell into the hands of mosstroopers and brigands, chiefly connected with the Liddesdale families of Scot, Elliot, Little, Trumble, and Armstrong. The thieves of Liddesdale and the outlaws of Leven they are generally termed in the Scottish annals, and their affiance was courted by the chiefs of Annandale in numerous civil feuds. This ground being claimed alternately by England and Scotland, became known as the Debateable Land; but, by a treaty in 1552, it was divided between the two kingdoms, and stone pillars set along the frontier to mark the boundary. The Irvings of Robgill and Bonshaw at this time occupied the Scottish territory nearest to the mouth of the Esk. William Johnstone of Gretna and Newbie mortgaged Sarkbrig and Conheath to Richard Irving, and leased Stapleton to Christopher Irving of Bonshaw, whose son married Margaret, daughter of Johnstone of that Ilk. There were one or two more marriages between the Irvings and Johnstones of Newbie and of Johnstone, so that the Irvings acquired a "kyndlie"—i.e., a kinsman's right to live in the barony of Newbie without title-deeds. Their name early appears among the followers of Robert Bruce; and Dick Irving, a notorious freebooter, was captured by the English in 1527. His relations retaliated by seizing Geoffrey Middleton, a connection of Lord Dacre, the English Warden, on his return from a pilgrimage to St. Ninian's in Galloway; and in spite of the object of his journey, which by the rules of regular warfare ought to have protected him, they kept him in prison till Lord Dacre should ransom him by releasing Dick Irving. Christie Irving of Bonshaw, Cuthbert Irving of Robgill, the Irvings of Pennersach, Wat Irving, and Jeffrey Irving surrendered to the English in 1547 with 290 retainers. They have direct male descendants.

Charteris of Amisfield is an ancient family, of which the head—the Earl of Wemyss and March—has now passed out of Dumfriesshire. The first of the name came to England with the Conqueror, and, like the Riddels, entered Scotland with David I. Robert de Charteris acquired the lands of Amisfield prior to 1175, and his grandson Thomas made over the patronage of two churches in Dumfriesshire to the Monastery of Kelso. In 1517 John Charteris of Amisfield was "caution for Ninian Crichton in his tutory to Margaret Crichton." Another Laird of Amisfield (or Hempisfield) acted with Sir Alexander Stewart of Garlies as prolocutor for Sir William Maxwell of Gribton, Barbara Johnstone, his wife, and Elizabeth Stewart, Barbara's mother, the widow of the deceased Laird of Newbie, when they were tried in 1605 for violently seizing Newbie Castle from Robert Johnstone; and in 1637 John Johnstone, called of Mylnefield (Robert's nephew), twice acted as sole witness to a sasine for Sir John Charteris. The Lairds of Amisfield are mentioned in most public transactions in Dumfriesshire in the 16th and 17th centuries.

The family of Fitz-Alleyne owned lands in Nithsdale long before any of them ascended the Scottish throne; but when the son of Walter, High Steward of Scotland, afterwards Robert II., took the surname of Stuart, they followed his example. [The English Stewards claim descent from Sir John Stewart of Bonkill.] The Stewarts of Garlies and the Stuarts of Castlemilk are of this race. Sir Walter Stewart of Dalswinton acquired Garlies, in Kirkcudbright, about the time of Robert Bruce, and his direct descendant, Sir Alexander Stewart, was created Earl of Galloway in 1623.

The Fergussons of Craigdarroch are also an ancient family. The first charter in existence of their estate is dated early in the 14th century, and they are supposed to have possessed it for many years previously. Burns refers to them in these words—

Thy line that have struggled for freedom with Bruce,
Shall heroes and patriots ever produce.

The poet's great friend to whom this was addressed was Robert Fergusson, also a poet, who died in his 24th year, in 1751. Burns wrote the inscription on his monument in the Canongate Churchyard, in Edinburgh—

No sculptured marble here, nor pompous lay,
No storied urn, nor animated bust—
This simple stone directs Pale Scotia's way
To pour her sorrows o'er her poet's dust.

Comparatively few of the Dumfriesshire landed gentry descend in the male line from the ancestors who owned their property in the 15th and 16th centuries, but among them appear to be the Hunters of Lagan, who received the estate from Robert Bruce. They are now represented by Mr Hunter-Arundell of Barjarg Tower, near Dumfries. The Hope-Johnstones of Annandale descend through two females from the first Marquis. The Charterises are now Charteris Douglas, while other families which have died out in the male branch have still retained the ancient name with the female descent.

The Griersons of Lag have continued in the male line from Gilbert, second son of Malcolm Dominus de MacGregor, who died in 1374. They were created baronets in the 17th century, and intermarried with the Maxwells, Charterises, Kirkpatricks, Fergussons, and Queensberry family. Lag Castle stands about seven miles from Dumfries, and, like Lochwood, was built in the midst of morasses and thick woods. Sir Alexander Grierson of Lag, born 1858, is the head of this ancient family.

Lag Castle

The Norman family of Heris, descended from the Count de Vendôme, came to England with the Conqueror, and followed David I. to Scotland, where Robert de Heris is called Dominus de Nithsdale in a charter of 1323. As Herries of Terregles they played a prominent part in Scottish history, and finally merged into the Maxwells. The title of Herries was created in 1489; and the family of Constable Maxwell, Everingham Park, Co. York, established their claim to it through female descent in 1858. The present Lord Herries, born 1837, has two daughters.

The Herries family owned Hoddom Castle, where they are said to have imprisoned kidnapped Englishmen in the 15th century, but in 1607 it belonged to Samuel Kirkpatrick, married to the widow of Johnstone of Newbie. It was bought about 1630 by the Sharps, and remained with their descendants till the present day. Charles Kirkpatrick Sharpe, the celebrated antiquarian, whom Sir Walter Scott called the Scottish Horace Walpole, and the author of several poems in the Border Minstrelsy, was born there in 1781, and died in Edinburgh in 1851.

The Maitlands of Eccles are an old Scottish house, descending from Eklis or Elsie, a knight who followed the fortunes of Hugh de Morville into Dumfriesshire in the reign of David I. The office and estates of the Morvilles descended to the M'Dowalls.

The Boswells of Auchinleck are described as minor barons in 1549, and have produced eminent advocates and a judge. Perhaps the best known of the family is James Boswell, the friend and biographer of Dr Samuel Johnson, whose life he published in 1791.

The Clark-Kennedys now represent the family of the old Celtic Thanes of Carrick. The name Dunwiddie of Applegarth often occurs in history, and is derived from Alleyn Dinwithie, whose name appears in the Ragman's Roll. The Bells of Middlebie and of Blacket House, in the parish of Kirkpatrick-Fleming, were a numerous race, and their chiefs surrendered to the English in 1547, with 364 men. The Romes were a small clan living under the protection of the Johnstones in Gretna, in the 16th century, but subsequently increased their fortunes and estates. For a time they possessed the Castle of Dalswinton, which was given by Robert Bruce to his son-in-law's kinsman, Sir Walter Stewart.

Chapter Six

In January, 1461, Queen Margaret, wife of the deposed King Henry VI. of England, came with her son, Edward Prince of Wales, to Dumfries to seek allies against her husband's rival, the Duke of York. The Queen Mother of Scotland met her on the Borders, and, according to the chronicler of Auchinleck, a marriage was projected between young Edward and an infant Scottish Princess; but the Prince perished the same year by the sword of Richard, the Duke of Gloucester, after the battle of Tewkesbury, and the Royal House of York was eventually acknowledged by James III.

The second Douglas rebellion was hardly crushed in 1484 when a third broke out under another of the Douglases, Archibald Earl of Angus. Dumfriesshire was again the scene of strife, and the insurgent lords adopted the cruel expedient of bringing the young James, Prince of Scotland, into the field against his father, and by this means drawing many who would otherwise have been loyal or neutral under the rebel standard. At the battle of Sauchieburn, June 1488, the royal troops were routed. James III. fled wounded from the field, and took refuge in a cottage, where he was murdered by a straggler in the guise of a priest, whom the frightened owner of the house had brought in, as she thought, to hear the confession of the dying monarch. Lord Maxwell had been nominally on the side of the King, yet contrived to gain the favour of his opponents, and was appointed to rule Dumfriesshire with Lord Angus till the Prince of Scotland should attain his majority, he being at this time not sixteen years of age. Adam, laird of Johnstone, was on the King's side. He was first cousin to Maxwell, and had married a Scot of Branxholme and Buccleuch. A precept of sasine from Patrick, Earl of Bothwell, in 1493, "to our lovit, Adam of Johnstone of that Ilk and others, charges them to infeft Walter Scot of Buccleuch in the lands of Roberthill, in the Stewartry of Annandale." The Scots, whose descendant, the Duke of Buccleuch, had a rental of £79,000 from Dumfriesshire ten years ago, do not appear to have possessed an acre of land there before 1459. Some of the clan were very troublesome a little later to the public peace, and in 1514 joined the English Warden in a raid on Dumfriesshire. But in 1569, during the civil war between the unfortunate Queen Mary and her third husband, Bothwell, and the Protestant party under the Regent and infant James VI., "the barons, landit men, and gentlemen, inhabitants of the Sheriffdom of Berwick, Roxburgh, Selkirk, and Peebles," signed a bond to support the young King. It was dated at Kelso, April 6, headed by the name of Buccleuch, Knt., and followed by many Scots, Kers, Cranstanes, Gledstanes, and others. They professed themselves specially enemies to all persons named Armstrong, Elliot, Nickson, Little, Beattie, Thomson, Irving, Bell, Johnstone, Glendinning, Routlege, Henderson, and Scott of Ewisdale—in fact, of those families who had fought on the side of the Queen at Langholm. Nevertheless, the same year a decreet sentenced Sir Walter Scot of Branxholme to arrest and confiscation for having forfeited his caution; but probably this stern sentence was never carried out, as at that time and much later the decreets of the Edinburgh Courts were little more than a form as regarded the Border gentry. For a much graver offence Jeffrey Irving was condemned to be executed, without effect. The Scots of Buccleuch were high in favour with James VI., and were raised to the peerage three years after the union of the two Crowns. At that period many of the Gordons, Scots, and Johnstones entered the Dutch and other foreign services, for when peace became permanent between England and Scotland the land on the Borders would not support them all, and they were unfitted for civil occupations. Scot of Buccleuch received a sum of money from the Prince of Orange, whose son afterwards married a daughter of Charles I., for the mosstroopers and cattle-drivers from the middle marches whom he despatched to fight against Holland's enemies.

The manner in which the Dumfries chiefs defied the law was shown in 1509, when Lord Crichton, the Sheriff, held an assize in Dumfries, and Lord Maxwell, the Warden of the Borders, on account of some private feud, came with a body of armed men, including some of the Johnstones, and what the chroniclers call a great battle was fought outside. The young Lairds of Dalziell and Crauchlay, besides Robert Crichton, the Sheriff's near relation (himself an outlaw), were killed. Four years later Maxwell and his four brothers fell at the battle of Flodden, which again left Scotland with a boy-king in 1513. An Irving of Bonshaw, Lord Herries of Terregles, with his brother Andrew, and many Dumfries gentlemen, besides their followers, were among the slain, and the defeat was at once followed up by an English raid into the county under Lord Dacre, who induced some of the Armstrongs, Grahames, and Scots to join him. He wrote to the Privy Council that he had almost depopulated Lower Annandale and Eskdale, that he had destroyed 400 ploughed lands, that no man was dwelling in any of them at this day, save only in the towns of Annan, Steppel, and Wauchope, and that he means to continue his forays from time to time, to the utmost annoyance of the Scots.

It is not surprising, after this savage treatment, that the ruined and probably half-starved borderers did not adhere very strictly to the treaty between England and France, in which Scotland was included, in 1515. The Queen Mother, sister to Henry VIII., had married the young Archibald, Earl of Angus, very soon after her husband's death at Flodden, so the Scottish nobles, jealous of his elevation, deprived her of the government for her son, and John, Duke of Albany, first cousin to James IV., was appointed regent. Lord Dacre complained that he at once discharged the Border officers put in by the Queen and replaced them by unfit persons, which had caused great disorder. He said that nine Englishmen had been murdered by Scotsmen, and great robberies and burnings committed, for which no redress can be obtained. Albany had sent Lord Lindsay, the Laird of Bass, and Sir Wm. Scot to the Borders to meet the English Warden, when a demand was made of redress for the murder of Robert Dalgles, his son, and David Tate, Scotsmen, and of Henry Milne, Englishman; and, though one of the murderers was present in sight of the Warden and Commissioners, his delivery was refused.

The Warden again wrote to Albany, who held out hope of redress, but immediately afterwards three more Dalglieshes and John Oliver Jackson of Rowcliff were killed by the young laird of Gretna, assisted by two of the Irvings and Peter Grahame. Again, an Englishman was killed by two of the Irvings, and two Bells. The Scotsmen who were among the murdered had all assisted the English in the recent foray; so probably their assassins looked upon it as a just retribution, even if they were not secretly instigated by the Government.

On November 27, 1515, Lord Dacre writes that the Warden of the Scottish Borders, with Lord Carlyle, Sir John Murray of Cockpool, the Laird of Johnstone, Symon Carruthers of Mouswald, Sir Alexander Jardine (comptroller of the Duke of Albany's house), Carruthers of Holmains, Charteris of Amisfield, William Johnstone of Gretna, Dunwiddie, the Lairds of Knock, Castlemilk, Kirkconnel, Tinwald, and others, came to Solam Chapel in England, where the said Warden "sent forth in a scrymage" the Laird of Johnstone, Captain of Lochmaben, and others to the number of 400 horses and more. They came to Arthuret in the Duchy of Lancaster, burnt a Grange and. a whole village to the number of 16 houses. Returning to Scotland the Warden sent forth "in another scrymage to Sir John Murray, Laird of Cockpool, Sir Alexander Jardine, the Laird of Mansfield, Amisfield, Tynewald, the Provost of. Dumfries, and others to the number of 700 horsemen, who robbed Bowness, and burnt 18 houses with much corn, hay, &c., assaulted the tower and barnekyn for half an hour and returned."

On May 15, 1517, Albany gave a respite "to the Armstrongs, Tailors, and all their kinsmen, friends, servants, and. other dependents on them of the clan Liddisdale, now dwelling in the Debateable Lands and Woods, that will deliver to the governor (Albany) sufficient pledges to remain for good rule where they shall be assigned." The disturbed state of the country is shown by the numerous bonds of manrent, as they were termed, or agreements for mutual

Amisfield

protection, entered into at this period. Brothers formed them with brothers, and the Laird of Johnstone being an outlaw engaged himself in this way to Maxwell in 1528. The year before James V. declared in Parliament his utter ignorance of a raid that the Laird of Johnstone had lately made up to the walls of Carlisle. In June, 1528, the Laird of Johnstone and Edward Maxwell, the Warden's brother, burnt houses and corn fields in Annandale, besides some of the Royal woods at Drumscore, in consequence of which and of similar exploits Lord Maxwell, Lord Bothwell, Lord Home, Scot of Buccleuch, Mark Ker of Fernihurst, and Johnstone were cited before the Parliament, which held its session in the Tolbooth at Edinburgh, May 16, 1529, where they were at once arrested, and shut up in the Castle. Leaving them there the King set out on July 26 with 8000 men to Dumfriesshire. He biletted a large portion of these troops on the Deputy Warden, Charteris of Amisfield, because he had taken no steps to procure the release of a youth seized near Lochmaben by a party of Englishmen, who had also carried off two cows, the only other possession of his widowed mother; and she had made her way on foot to Stirling to lay her complaint before the King; but if report spoke truly of the way in which James obtained possession of the Laird of Gilnockie, Johnnie Armstrong, it was not quite so creditable to him. This rebel had only three years before met Lord Maxwell at Dumfries and tendered his submission, for which he had obtained a grant of land at Langholm, and now received an autograph letter from James V. asking him to meet him near Hawick, and promising him a pardon. Armstrong went richly attired with 24 splendidly accoutred horsemen, at sight of which the King exclaimed, "What wants yon knave that a king should have," and ordered them all to be hung on the neighbouring trees. Armstrong's wife and daughters are said to have mistrusted the King's letter, and to have tried to induce him to remain in his own strong tower. The King had already captured Adam Scot of Tushielaw, commonly known as the Prince of Thieves, and had him promptly hanged. On his return to Edinburgh, James released the Border chiefs, and Johnstone shortly afterwards gained his favour by capturing George Scot of the Bog, a freebooter noted for his cruelty, whom the King ordered to be burnt alive. [A penalty with previous torture, enforced as late as 1789 in Berlin and Vienna.] This punishment seems to have been then unknown in Scotland, as a contemporary chronicler relates that everyone was astonished at it. These executions were undoubtedly in consequence of the complicity of the culprits in the English invasions, not for mere brigandage and theft.

In spite of the bond of manrent between the lairds, Dacre wrote to Cardinal Wolsey in 1528 that "the Debateable land is now clear waste," from the Maxwell and Johnstone feuds, and on April 2, 1529, he says "the Lord Maxwell caused the Armstrongs to make a raid upon the Lord of Johnstone, his own sister's son, who is at deadly feud with them for the killing of Mickle Armstrong, where they killed three of his friends and the Lord Maxwell himself lay in abushment to maintain them, purposely to have killed the said Lord of Johnstone if he had pursued them." Wharton, who succeeded as Warden of the English Borders, wrote to Henry VIII. in 1542 that Lochinvar (Gordon) and the Johnstones are the greatest enemies Maxwell had, owing to their wish to supplant him in the offices he held as Warden of the East and West Borders— one in Galloway, and the other in Annandale.

The Johnstones were now the chief proprietors in the part of Scotland most exposed to England. The Laird's estates extended northward to Moffat and beyond. His brother Adam was Baron of Corry. Another brother (James) was laird of Wamphray. William Johnstone of Gretna owned the barony of Newbie, including Stapleton, the salt works of Saltcoats, Gretna, and the fisheries from the Annan to the Eden; and the laird's estates intersected William's in Kirkpatrick-Fleming, and connected William's properties of Stapleton and Newbie by Broomhills. There were also Bells and Irvings dependents on the house of Johnstone and Newbie (it is stated in a legal process of 1611) who lived in the barony of Newbie without paying any dues, doubtless for the price of their services against invaders; so that as the Johnstones formed a cordon along the frontier, guarded the ford over the Esk, and suffered the most from English raids, they considered they had more claim to the office of Warden than Maxwell, whose original property lay to the east of the Lochar, and the frontier was never better guarded than when the Laird of Johnstone held the post. When Maxwell was Warden Ninian Crichton of Sanquhar was cited before a Justiciary Court for not giving assistance, and he answered that it had never been the duty of Sanquhar to protect the Borders. In 1540, the Laird of Johnstone and Sir Walter Scott of Branxholme were imprisoned at Dumbarton through Maxwell's influence, but released on parole on the security of Adam Johnstone of Corry, the Laird's brother. Two years before, Johnstone's estate had been sequestrated on the occasion of a second visit which James V. paid to Dumfriesshire, when Maxwell was rewarded with the confiscated Armstrong estates in Eskdale. Johnstone's were not restored till 1542-3, when he made a charter of resignation in favour of his son.

The marriage of James IV. with the daughter of Henry VII. had not produced the long peace which was expected between the two countries, and Dumfriesshire never endured more disasters than between the Battle of Flodden and the death of James V. The Reformation was also beginning to make its way into Scotland, and following the precedent of other countries the first adherents of it were condemned to the stake. William Johnstone was one of the Dumfries Commissioners for trying heretics. August 26, 1534. James V. had been favourably disposed towards the Reformers till the pressure of his uncle Henry VIII. to make him throw off the Papal supremacy, and Henry's persecution of the Romanists, disinclined him to them; and from this time "the Defender of the Faith" evidently courted a war with Scotland. In 1541 his army made an inroad into Dumfriesshire, and several Border lairds who hitherto had been out of favour with James were rewarded. for their valour in repelling it. William Johnstone of Gretna and Newbie was made a hereditary Baron for "good, faithful, and gratuitous service," and his lands entailed on his heirs male, or, in default of heirs male, to heirs of his own name bearing the arms of Johnstone. Jan. 2, 1542. James vainly applied to Henry VIII. for an indemnity for this foray, and then raised an army of 10,000 men under Lord Huntly. He came to Dumfries to inspect his troops, and Sir Thomas Wharton, the English Warden, proposed to Henry VIII. that as his nephew had but a small escort he should be seized and brought across the Border just as 260 years later the Spanish Princes were seized by Napoleon. The King was highly pleased with the idea, but when it was put before the Privy Council they raised these objections in a written reply—"They should have feared," said the document, "to have thought on such a matter touching a King's person had not their Royal master told them to do so. But, sir," it continued, "we have also weighed the matter, after our own simple wits and judgments, and we find in it many difficulties. First, the Castle of Caerlaverock, whereunto he resorts, is twenty miles within the ground of Scotland. We consider also that the country between that and England is so well inhabited that it would be very difficult to convey any such number of men to the place where he should be intercepted, but the same would be discovered. We consider again that Dumfries, one of the best towns in Scotland, is in that part where the enterprise should be done, and the country so inhabited at their backs that it would be hard to bring him thence, especially alive." It referred to the slander and deadly feud which would accrue if the plan failed, and advised that Wharton should let no creature know that it had ever been thought of.

Foiled in this project, Henry despatched an army of 10,000 men to the East Marches, and the banished Earl of Angus and his brother accompanied it.

They were defeated by Lord Huntly at Haddon Rig, and retaliated by burning Kelso and other Border towns, but James checked them in person at Falamuir, and wished to follow the fugitives into England in the hope of capturing the Duke of Norfolk, their commander, who when Earl of Surrey had conquered James IV. at Flodden. But the Border Lords refused to give their consent to this movement, and their withdrawal was fatal to it. They would defend their own frontiers, but would not expend the blood of their followers in a brilliant feat of arms to add lustre to a sovereign who had by turns humiliated them all, even his favourite Maxwell. Maxwell did offer to collect an army of his own followers in Dumfriesshire, and lead them on to Carlisle, which was not the untried ground to them that a march from the East Borders seemed to be; but the King, angry and discontented, retired to Maxwell's castle at Carlaverock, and while allowing him to suppose that he was to have the chief command in this new expedition, secretly bestowed it on Oliver Sinclair, a gentleman of his household, who first exhibited his commission (according to Holinshed, 1576) when the army was in face of the English. "As soon as that was read," says this author, "the Earls and Lords there present thought themselves debased too much to have such a mean gentleman advanced in authority above them all, and determined not to fight under such a captain, but willingly suffered themselves to be overcome, so were taken by the English without slaughter of any one person on either side." Sir Thomas Wharton in his report states that twenty Scotch were slain and some drowned, but not ten English were missing. "There be taken four falconets with three of J. R., and the arms of Scotland with an imperial crown upon every one of them; besides some hagbuts, axes, and handguns." He gives this list of "Noblemen and Gentlemen of Scotland taken prisoners upon Esk and thereabouts, by the King's highness's subjects, on Friday, November 24th."

"The Earl of Cassillis, [The son of this Earl of Cassillis was the infamous chief who half-roasted the lay Abbot of Crossraguel before a slow fire to induce him to sign away the abbey lands in his own behalf, a property which the family of Kennedy still enjoyed (and probably do so still) in 1832, when Scott borrowed the first part of the incident for his scene in Ivanhoe between Front-de-Boeuf and the Jew Isaac.] the Earl of Glencairn, Lord Maxwell, Admiral of Scotland, and Warden of the West Marches; Lord Fleming of the Council, Lord Somerville of the Council, Lord Oliphant, Lord Gray, Oliver Sinclair of the King's Privy Council, and three of his brothers; John Ross, Lord of Craigie and Gentleman Usher of the King of Scots' Privy Chamber; Robert Erskine, son and heir of Lord Ersine, late Ambassador; Seton, son-in-law to Lord Erskine; George Hume, Laird of Hayton; Walter Kerr, Laird of Gordon; John Charteris, uncle and keeper to Lord Amisfield in his minority; David Gordon, bastard uncle to Lochinvar; Lord Langton, Lord Monteith, John Maxwell, brother to Lord Maxwell; and Master Johnstone, [This was the oldest son of the Laird of Johnstone, not the Laird himself, and he was probably the sister's son of Maxwell referred to elsewhere.] John Leslie of Fife, bastard son to the Earl of Rothes; John Maitland, Larid of Aukincastle; Robert Charteris, the Lord of

Amisfield's brother; Master David Keith; John Melville, James Pringle, chief scorer of the King's goods, and in his favor. I think there are about a thousand prisoners, whereof two hundred be gentlemen." A supplementary list of the resources of the prisoners, gives "Lord Maxwell, in lands per annum," as worth "a thousand marks, sterling (English), and in goods, £500, which is £2000 Scotch. Henry Maxwell, his brother, in lands per annum nothing, in goods nothing." Another list contains the pledges delivered to the Earl of Cumberland and Sir Thomas Wharton at Carlisle, on January 19th, 1543; which corrects a previous memorandum. "For the Earl of Cassillis—Davie and Archibald his brothers, having no brother called Arthur as the schedule is; and the Laird of Cove. For the Laird of Glencarne—Alexander, his eldest son, and Robert, another son. For Lord Fleming—James, his son and heir, and John Fleming, called the young Laird of Roghall, otherwise called the Laird How in the schedule, with a Schoolmaster. For Lord Somerville— James, his eldest son, and Roger Maitland, his brother-in-law. For Lord Maxwell—Robert Maxwell, his son and heir. For Lord Oliphant—no pledge is coming, but himself remains." The same is said of Lord Gray, and of Oliver Sinclair and his two brothers. Oliver had been captured by a certain Willie Bell. "For the Laird of Craigie—Thomas Ross, his eldest son; he hth no such brother's son as the schedule purports, and the Nobleman saith his eldest son was his pledge. For Lord Darcy— John Monteith, his uncle's son and heir; he has no eldest son as the schedule purports; this is the same as the Nobleman said was appointed for his pledge—t.c. all the said Noblemen of their honours stand bound that all prisoners whose pledges entered not shall truly remain within the city of Carlisle unto such time as further orders shall be taken with them," t.c.

The King at Carlaverock heard of the rout at Solway Moss, and never recovered from the shock. He retired to Falkland, where he shut himself up, and would see no one, till the news arrived that the Queen had given birth to a daughter. He had been unfortunate in his domestic relations, for his first wife had died within a year of their marriage, and his second wife had lost two sons on the same day—James, aged a year and a half, and Arthur, aged a few months; and this infant being a girl, seemed to complete his disappointments. He said that Henry would now certainly try to obtain Scotland by marriage or some other means. "It was reported," says Holinshed, "that he was disquieted with some unkindly medicine, but howsoever the matter was, he yielded up his spirit to Almighty God on December 13th, 1542," at the age of thirty-two. The Earl of Arran, his cousin, was appointed Regent for the infant Queen.

This event produced a change on the Borders. Henry would not accept a pledge for Lord Maxwell, who was removed with the principal prisoners to Hampton Court; and the new Governor of Scotland at once restored the Laird of Johnstone's property. Feb. 27, 1543. A royal charter dated three days later declares that the Queen, in consideration of the good, faithful, and gratuitous service rendered by John Johnstone of that Ilk on the Borders of Scotland, grants to him in free tenement or life-rent, and to James Johnstone, his son and heir apparent, and his heirs heritably, all the lands of Johnstone, &c., to be created and incorporated into one entire and free Barony, to be called and comprehended within the Barony of Johnstone. This was the first dignity bestowed on the direct ancestor of the Marquises of Annandale; and was granted in precisely the same terms as the Barony of Newbie to William Johnstone the previous year.

Directly he heard of his nephew's death, Henry VIII., as James had anticipated, began to think of marrying his young son Edward to the orphaned Mary, and he released the imprisoned Scottish nobles on condition that they would do their best to promote it. Finding this impossible, they returned to captivity; and alarmed by a threat that he would be transferred to the Tower, Maxwell asked to be removed instead to a prison at Carlisle, "to the intent that he might practise on his son and his sister's son, the Laird of Johnstone" (i.e., the Laird's eldest son James, who was imprisoned there), and he proposed "to deliver up any castle of his own that was commodious to the King for entering into Scotland;" but Henry also required the Royal Castle of Lochmaben to give him a permanent hold on Dumfriesshire.

Lord Hertford, writing to Paget, July 29th, 1545, describes Maxwell as worn by vexation and imprisonment, and unable to drink, eat, or sleep, that he was ready to serve as a red-cross English soldier if required; but in short, that if once shut up in the Tower, he knew "he should never return on leave." While negotiations were going on for the surrender of Lochmaben and Carlaverock, the Master of Maxwell, Lord Maxwell's eldest son, was taken prisoner, and the second son, John (afterwards Lord Herries), refused to listen to any treacherous scheme. Wharton wrote to Lord Shrewsbury, Feb. 14, 1545, that he had placed a body of foot and a troop of fifty horse in Langholm Tower (belonging to the Armstrongs), and had long used one of Johnstone's followers as an emissary to create discord between Johnstone and Maxwell's son. A feud had broken out between them which the Scotch Privy Council could not allay. He had offered 300 crowns to Johnstone for himself, and 100 to his brother the Abbot of Saulsyde, and 100 to Johnstone's other followers, on condition that the Master of Maxwell should be put into his power. Johnstone had entered into the plot, but "he and his friends were all so false" that Wharton knew "not what to say." But he would "be glad to annoy and entrap the Master of Maxwell or the Laird of Johnstone to the King's Majesty's honor and his own poor honesty."

The Abbot of Saulsyde was a Johnstone, but was possibly not brother to the Laird, for the English Wardens often confused relationships and Christian names, when they described the Border families, with their numerous members bearing the same surnames; and an additional difficulty was caused by the custom of giving the same Christian name occasionally to brothers. In the Johnstone family alone, the old Laird had two brothers besides himself called John; he had two sons named John and two named James; and William of Newbie had also two sons named John.

Hertford, in a letter to the Privy Council, gives Sir Thomas Wharton's opinion as to the ease of an attack on Carlaverock. He had already advised the burning of Gretna and Redkirk, and his description of the country shows how much it had suffered since the foray in 1536, and since the capture of James V. had been discussed in 1541.

"He saith that upon the West Marches of Scotland, the country of itself being wild and desolate, there is no exploit to be done nearer than Dumfries, except to make a raid in to overthrow and cast down a certain church and steeple, called the Steeple of Annan, which is a thing of little importance; and to go to Dumfries, he saith the country is so strong by nature, and the passages there so straight and narrow, that he thinketh it over hard and dangerous to be tried with a Warden's rode. The West Marches being barren, and already wasted by the continuance of wars, &c. He describes the swamps surrounding Carlaverock, and the difficulty of passing them. But a month or two later this was overcome, and a Scottish diary of the time records (October 28, 1545)—"The Lord Maxwell delivereth Carlaverock to the English, which was great discomfort to the country." Three days afterwards Carlaverock was surrounded by Johnstone, Douglas of Drumlanrig, and Gordon of Lochinvar, but it was not recaptured till May, 1546; and in the meantime, Lochmaben and Thrieve had been surrendered to the English by the Earl of Arran, Regent of Scotland, who pardoned Maxwell's treachery, and restored him to the Wardenship. Maxwell died July 9, 1546, having bequeathed one important legacy to his country in an Act he introduced into Parliament during his short release on parole in 1543, and which was passed after some opposition—viz., to "make it lawful for all our Sovereign Lady's lieges to possess and read copies of the Bible in Scottish or English." The Act may be said to have legally introduced the Reformed Faith into Scotland.

Early in 1547, Johnstone, Lochinvar, and the Master of Maxwell made a raid into Cumberland, but the next month Sir Thos. Carleton crossed the frontier—not at the usual ford, but at Canonby—and pushed on to Dumfries, whence he proclaimed that all who did not take an oath of allegiance to the King of England should be pursued with fire and sword. Some of the Lairds of Nithsdale and Galloway gave pledges of fidelity to the English. He states that Canonby was now far from the enemy, for all Annandale, Liddesdale, and a great part of Nithsdale and Galloway were willing to submit, except the Laird of Drumlanrig, who never submitted, and with him Alexander Carlyle, the Laird of Bridekirk, and his son Adam, the young Laird—so he tried to get some castle where he might be nearer the enemy. "Sander Armstrong came and told me he had a man called John Lynton, who was born in the head of Annandale, near to the Loughwood, being the Laird Johnstone's chief house, and the said Laird and his brother (being the Abbot of Saulside) were taken prisoners not long before, and were remaining in England. It was a fair large tower, able to lodge all our company safely, with a barne-kin hall, kitchen, and stables, all within the barne-kin, and was but kept with two or three fellows and as many wenches."

This garrison was easily overpowered, and the place found to be well stocked with salted beef, malt, butter, and cheese. Carleton put Armstrong in the tower to keep it, and then proceeded to Moffat, where he ordered the people to swear allegiance to Edward. VI. The treacherous Armstrongs and Fergus Grahame offered to show him the road into Lanarkshire, hitherto untrodden by the enemy, "for at Crawford and Lamington he would find much booty and many sheep." He burned "Lamington and James Douglas's castle, where the men and cattle were all devoured with smoke and fire," and then returned to Lochwood, or Loughwood, an isolated tower standing on a hill in the midst of marshes, which could only be crossed by strangers with a guide, and there he writes in his own narrative of these proceedings. "We remained very quietly, as if we had been at home in our own houses."

While these events were passing in Dumfriesshire an English army was ravaging East Lothian and Teviotdale, and, encouraged by its success in fire and slaughter, Lord Lennox and Wharton, who had been ennobled, crossed the Esk, Sept. 8, 1547, to subdue the South of Annandale, which still resisted their lieutenant. They halted at Gretna, and marched next day to Castlemilk, which they reported had walls 14 feet thick, and captured it. On Sept. 20 they encamped near Annan, and summoned Lyon, the commander of the Castle, who defended it with 100 Scots, to surrender, which he refused. The Castle was built by Robert Bruce, and the chapel adjoining it was the only Church in Annan. It stood in the midst of the old graveyard, where all that remains of the fortress is a small heap of stones. "The English," wrote Holinshed, "brought their artillery to bear against the walls, and undermine them with powder, so that the roof of the church was shaken down and many of those within crushed to death. At last the Captain, moved by the Earl of Lennox, to whom he claimed to be of kin, rendered the steeple unto him, with himself and 96 Scottish soldiers, with condition to have their lives saved, and the captain to go a prisoner to England. Immediately they came forth of the steeple, fire was set to the mines, and both church and steeple blown up into the air and razed to the ground. This done, they sacked and burnt the town, and left not a stone standing, for it had ever been a right noisome neighbour to England. The Englishmen had conceived such spite to it that if they saw but a piece of timber remaining unburnt, they would out the same in pieces. The country herewith was stricken in such fear that the next day all the Kilpatricks, and the Jardines, the Lairds of Kirkmichael, Aplegirth, Closeburn, Howmendes, Nuby, [Holinshed is usually very accurate. Except as Nuby, whom he evidently took to represent the clan, he mentions no Johnstones, though they formed the most numerous portion.] and the Irrewings, the Belles, the Rigges, the Murrays, and all the clans and the surnames of the nether part of Annandale, came and received an oath of obeisance as subjects to the King of England, delivering pledges for their assured loyalty." The invaders were again assisted by "Richie Grahame," and by some of the Armstrongs, Beatties, Thomsons, Littles, and other Border stragglers who were not dependent on any special chief.

In Bell's MS., preserved in the Carlisle Cathedral Library, there is a list of chiefs and their men who surrendered on this occasion to the English. It differs slightly from the two lists preserved among the State papers of Edward

VI., as do those two lists from each other, both as to names and the number of followers. In one the Laird of Wamphray is omitted, and the Gretna Johnstones mentioned twice. In the other Lord Carlile is mentioned twice with a different number of followers, but this sort of error occurs in all report of battles. The Laird of Johnstone and his son were both prisoners; but "William Johnstone, brother to the Laird of Johnstone, and his three brothers and those under them," are mentioned with 235 men. Robert Johnstone, the laird's second son, is mentioned in one list, but not in that now quoted—"George Johnstone, the Laird of Newbie, and those under him." This was the legitimized son of William Johnstone of Newbie, who succeeded to Gretna on his father's death. He had 37 men. "The Laird of Gretna," who may have been William's legitimate son John, who inherited Newbie, and those under him, 82, and Johnstones of Gretna, to the number of 11, had some time before served the English, probably by compulsion. Besides these, there was Sir John Lawson, chaplain to the Laird of Johnstone, with 32 men; the Johnstones of Lockerbie, of the Bank, and Foulduris, with 280 men; and Gawin Johnstone of Elsieschellis, with 38. The Laird of Gillisbe, with 72 men; 55 Jardines and Moffats, 104 Belles of Middlebie, 60 Nicksons, Hunters, and Glendinnings, 25 Carlyles, 80 Elliotts and Simpsons; the Armstrongs of Liddisdail, Ii Grahames, and 304 Beatties, Littles, and Thomsons—had all served the English; some above a year, some more than three years. The remaining names which surrendered on the capture of Annan were Christie Irving of Bonshaw, with 103 men; his nephew Christie, with 74; Richie and Wat Irving, with 149. The Romes of Tordoffe, with 26. The Johnstones of Craigeburn, Malinshaw, Cottes, and Drisdaill, with 306. The Belles of Middlebie, Kirkconnel, The Kirk, &c., with 302. Kirkpatrick of Closeburn, with 378; Grierson of Lag, with 360; the Laird of Kirkmichel, with 123; and the Laird Ross, with 86; the Laird of Cassilis, with 39; Edward Maxwell of Tinwald, with 81; the Jardines, with 341; John Maxwell of Brackenside and his brother, with 139; Charteris of Amisfield, with 111; Jeffrey Irving of Robgill, with 81; the Laird of Dunweddie, Patrick Murray, the Vicar of Caerlaverock, and others—the total amounting to about 6000 men. [Henry VIII. was now dead, and Lord Wharton wrote to the Lord Protector—"I have despatched both my sons, my son-in--law, Mr Musgrave, and other gentlemen with light horsemen to make a foray in Nithsdale, near Dumfries, and the part of Annandale not yet won. They have burnt nine or ten towns, and brought away prisoners and spoil of goods with no hurt. Since I last wrote 500 lairds and gentlemen have come in, and I have in all 2400 Scottish horse. . . I have removed Laird Johnston from Carlisle to my house at Wharton. All his men have refused him; his own brothers and others have taken oath and given hostages for their service. They are a great band of proper men, and do good service. . . . Laird Johnston is a good example upon these marches, for when his house was won and all his goods taken he requested to be sworn in the King's service."]

At the next session of Parliament in Edinburgh, June 12, 1584, the Lords declared the following chiefs, who had taken an oath on this occasion, to be guilty of high treason, and therefore outlawed:—"Willia Kirkpatrick of Kirkmichael; John Jardine of Aplegirth; John Carruthers of Holmends (he is mentioned in Bell's MS.);--of Ros; the Lairds of Knock, of Granton, and of Gillisbie; Grahame of Thornick; Gawyne of Johnstoun; of Kirktown; Jhonstoun of Craigeburn; James Jhonstoun of Cottis; -- of Newbie; Michael Lord Carlyle; Carruthers of Mouswald (mentioned in one of the two official lists); Cuthbert (it was Jeffrey) Irving of Robgill; —— of Cowquhate; Cuthbert Johnstoun of Lockerbie; James, sometime Abbot of Saulsyde; and Tweedie of Drumnelzear."

The capture of the Laird of Johnstone with similar acts of violence produced the following letter, written in the young Queen's name to Henry VIII., May 17th, 1547, not a month before the tyrant's end:—

"Right excellent, right high and mighty prince, our dearest brother and cousin, we in our most hearty manner recommend us unto you. Our dearest cousin and governor James, Earl of Arran, protector and governor of our realm, being lately advertised how our well beloved clerk, Master John Hay, sent to the most Christian King of France to perform such business as was committed unto him, and the Abbot of Dryburgh, who was passing to the ports of France in his own affairs, was not only invaded and taken on the sea by your ships and men of war, but are also holden within your realm as prisoners notwithstanding the comprehension in the peace taken by the most Christian King for we our realm and subjects of abstinence of war in both our realms openly proclaimed to stand betwixt the same and as yet undischarged. Also our said dearest cousin and tutor is advertised how your subjects have lately by open foray invaded our realm upon the West Borders, at the parts of Annandale, and there has taken the Laird of Johnstone on his own ground for defence of his lands and goods. The which unjust attempts are not only against the comprehension and abstinence foresaid, but also most unnaturally enterprised against us and our lieges without any respect unto the proximity and tenderness of our blood, and mutual friendship, that should continue between us and our realms. Therefore we pray you, our dearest brother and cousin, in our most effective manner to put the said Abbot of Dryburgh, Master John Hay, Lord Johnstone, and others taken with them to liberty and freedom, so that they may without any impediment from any of your subjects freely pass forward to the realm of France, or if it please them to return again within our realm, and it will please you give credence unto our trusty counsellor Sir Adam Otterburne, our ambassador in this behalf, t.c. We pray Almighty God to give you good and long life. Given at our Castle of Stirling, and subscribed by our dearest cousin, tutor and governor at Edinburgh, May 17th, and of our reign the 5th."

Henry seems to have become as anxious to annex Scotland before his death as his predecessor Edward I.; and the Duke of Norfolk was committed to the Tower, and his son beheaded, for their ill success at Fala Muir. The accession of Edward VI. was the signal for a still more determined and exterminating warfare than had already been carried on; and the letter just given was followed up by the Battle of Pinkie and Wharton's ravages in Annandale. The

Laird of Johnstone languished in prison at Pontefract Castle; and is described in the list of distinguished captures as "a gentleman of one hundred marks sterling or above, for whom the King's Majesty has paid one hundred marks in part payment for ransom to his taker; the Laird of Closeburn, worth £100 sterling and more, for whom his cousin Thomas Kirkpatrick was pledge; the Laird of Cockpool, a gentleman of £100 lands sterling or thereabouts, himself remains with Sir William Ingleby; and Cuthbert Murray, worth little or nothing."

The official list of the towns, monasteries, castles, villages, mills, and hospitals destroyed by the English in 1547 is given as two hundred and eighty-seven, and fills ten closely written pages of a State paper still preserved in the London Record Office.

Graitney, Sark, Cavartholme, Blacket House, Ryehill Castle, and all within fifteen miles of the English frontier are included, and Dumfriesshire was nominally subject to the King of England for a year and a half. But in the meantime the King of France sent a contingent to assist his Scotch allies, and hearing of this expected aid, the Privy Council gave orders to Wharton to execute some of the pledges at Carlisle, which was done, and among others who perished was the Warden of Grey Friars at Dumfries and the Vicar of Carlaverock, the last being pledge for Maxwell, and his near relation.

Considering the unprovoked nature of the war and the English excesses, it is not wonderful that when fortune turned in favour of the Scots, they retaliated with equal ferocity. The Chevalier Beaujeu, a French officer who served with them, and had been in Muscovy, so was enured to horrors, says that the English cruelties round Jedburgh "would have made to tremble the most savage Moor in Africa," and he gives a ghastly description of the vengeance which the Scotch wreaked on their unhappy prisoners. "I cannot," he adds, "greatly praise the Scotch for this practice, but the English tyrannised over the Borders in a most barbarous manner, and I think it was but fair to pay them in their own coin." The English, to counteract the French support, brought over a band of Germans and Italians, and a Spanish corps; and the actual peril in which the young Queen of Scotland was placed by the advance of the enemy upon Edinburgh, which was burnt, induced the Regent to send her to France in 1548, where she was educated and eventually married to the Dauphin Francis, who was henceforward in legal documents always styled King of Scotland. An attack of the French King upon Dunkirk and Calais, then belonging to England, compelled the English forces to withdraw from the south of Scotland, and a peace was finally arranged in 1551. This provided that the debateable land between the Esk and the Sark should lie waste and belong to neither kingdom, but by a supplementary article in 1552 it was divided; the upper half being adjudged to Scotland and the eastern part to England. The treaty is signed by John Johnstone of that Ilk; John Johnstone of Nitove (?); Charles Murray of Cockpool, and others. The younger Laird of Johnstone was dead; and it is a proof of the severity of a prison life at that period that few of the Scotch captives seem long to have survived their release. His widow, Margaret Hamilton, was married in 1552 to David Douglas of Coldbrandspeth.

Chapter Seven

One article of the Treaty of Peace in 1551 provided that there should be no marriages between natives of the Borders of England and those of Scotland; that no Borderer should pass from his own country to the other without a safe conduct; that no Scottish Borderer should ever sleep a night in Carlisle, and that there should be no trade between them. The object was to prevent quarrels which might lead to war. But the long hostilities had completely impoverished the south of Scotland, and stripped it of cattle, and the starving Borderers had more temptation than before to pillage their richer neighbours. While the treaty for the division of the Debateable Land was pending, Wharton writes that "the Lord Maxwell and Lord Johnstone, with 400 horsemen and a power of Scotland for 2000 men, came to the Debateable Land, but returned without doing harm, save that the Frenchmen burned a thatched cote house." He would not require a bond from the Warden of Scotland lest he should seem to acknowledge the Scotch authority over that district. John Maxwell was now Warden of the Scottish Borders. He is better known as Lord Herries, a title he obtained by his marriage with a cousin, the heiress of Terregles, and he resigned the office three years later on account of "diver's feuds" with some of the most notable families in these parts. The Book of Complaints, a MS.

Terregles

preserved in the Cathedral Library at Carlisle, contains the names of 400 offenders, who at different times made plundering forays into England. They probably extended over thirty or forty years, and included "Richie Grahame, younger of Netherby," many Bells, Grahames, several Johnstones, Gordons, Elliots, and other Border names; the young Laird of Graitney, Gordon of Graitney Hill, Edward Irving of Graitney Hill, David Johnstone of Robgill, &c., &c., who were specially reported to the Warden and Bishop of Carlisle; and were liable to be hung with little ceremony if captured. On the East Borders many of the chiefs, even those who had taken an oath to the King of England, were compensated for their losses after the war with the honour of knighthood, as the Lairds of Cessford, Fernihurst, Grenehead, Buccleuch, and others; but this dignity was conferred very sparingly in Dumfriesshire, though some of the chiefs had left that county rather than surrender to the English, and had lent their swords to resist the invaders of East Lothian and Edinburgh.

In 1455 a Royal Statute had commanded that 200 spearmen and as many archers should be maintained upon the East and Middle Marches of Scotland for their defence, and 100 spearmen and 100 archers upon the West Borders; also that "they who are near the Border are ordained to have good households and armed men as offers, and to be ready at their principal place, and to pass with the Wardens when and where they shall be charged;" but at the first Parliament, which met at Edinburgh after the peace of 1551, it was proposed that an annual tax should be levied instead for the purpose of keeping up a larger standing army. This was opposed by about 200 of the smaller Border chiefs, who assembled together in Edinburgh, and sent the Lairds of Calder and Wemyss to protest against any taxation, for they "would defend the realm as their forefathers had done," but had no money. They were soon put to the proof, for in 1557 an English army crossed the Borders of Scotland so suddenly that Lord Maxwell and other Scotch commissioners were still at Carlisle trying to arrange that peace should continue with England, in spite of a war which had just broken out between the English Queen Mary, on behalf of her husband Philip's dominions, and their French ally. Bothwell, afterwards husband to the Scottish Queen, was Lord of Liddesdale, and though on this occasion he was thrice defeated by the Armstrongs, he is said to have had more success against the English regular troops. As a Border chief he was courageous and humane. The principal leader among the Armstrongs, Sandie or Sander, who had acted as guide to the invaders in the last war, declared to the English Warden in 1550 that he "must become a Scotsman," if he was not protected against Lord Maxwell; but in 1557 Christopher Armstrong signed a bond of man-rent to "John Lord Maxwell, and Sir John Maxwell of Terregles (i.e., Lord Herries), Knt., his tutor and governor," in return for the gift "of the males of all and haill the lands which are contained in a bond made by the late John Armstrong, my father, to the late Robert, Lord Maxwell, gudsire (grandfather) to the said John, now Lord Maxwell." This John Armstrong was the chief summoned to pay homage to James V. in 1529, and who on appearing with 24 followers to meet the King during his passage to Dumfriesshire was taken and hung, a treacherous act, which disaffected all the Armstrongs towards the House of Stuart. An English Cumberland MS. of the 16th century says that they were very troublesome to England, but tolerated because at any time they could produce three hundred or four hundred men to oppose the Scots. Christopher's son Willie lived to equal his grandfather's fame, as a thief. James VI. made an expedition into Dumfriesshire in 1587 on purpose to capture him, but failed; and in 1596, when he was taken by the English and shut up in Carlisle Castle, Sir Walter Scot of Buccleuch led a party armed with ladders and other appliances from Sark or Morton, ten miles distant, scaled the walls of the fortress, and rescued him. The same year, some difficulty having arisen between the King and his Edinburgh subjects, there was a report that he meant to let loose Kinmont Willie (as Armstrong was called) and his followers upon the city. Immediately the shops were emptied and the wares placed in the strongest house in the town, while the owners armed and stood ready to defend them, for ten years, previously Buccleuch and Lord Home had led such a party into Stirling, and before they left it not even an iron grating remained upon any of the windows.

Peace was concluded between England and Scotland in 1559, and the young Queen, now a widow, returned from France two years later in the midst of the distractions caused by the Reformers and their opponents. A Reformation was, indeed, needed in Scotland, where the King's illegitimate son had been made Archbishop of St. Andrews when a few months old, and the revenues of abbeys and churches were bestowed on court favourites and sold to laymen as a provision for their younger sons. John Johnstone, Laird of Newbie (1565-76), bought the living of Dornock, and seems to have inherited the living of Kirkpatrick-Fleming. He bequeathed the last to his second son Robert, who was a married layman and adhered to Romanism; and in March 1595 there is a decreet in the Register of the Privy Council against James Johnstone of Dunskellie (the laird), Robert Johnstone, [He was uncle to the laird.] Laird of Newbie, and Charles Murray of Cockpool, for having their children baptised by a Jesuit priest. The towns of Dumfries and Sanquhar welcomed the Reformation, and Lord Herries had early ranged himself on that side, even joining Murray in opposing the Queen's unfortunate marriage with Darnley in 1565, on the ground that it was prejudicial to the Protestant interests. But his devotion to Queen Mary, who gave him the title of Herries on the baptism of her son James, made him revert to the support of the Roman party When it became a question of Mary and her enemies as much as of religion; and the Border families long adhered to Romanism.

Among the records of Criminal Trials for 1572 at Dumfries, June 26th, appears that of "John Johnstone, commonly called Sir John Johnstone, commendator (i.e., Abbot) of Saulsyde," convicted of celebrating mass "after the Papistical manner." Symon Johnstone and John Johnstone of Kellobank were his securities. The same Abbot had been found guilty of fire-raising two years earlier, and laying waste the house and lands of Robert Johnstone of Craigaburn.

On the 20th of August, 1563, Queen Mary visited Dumfries for the first time, and passed a night under Lord Herrie's roof. She came again with her second husband, Henry Darnley, in 1565, from Edinburgh, halting a night at Lanark and Crawford on their road. Two years later she was consigned a prisoner to Lochleven Castle suspected, probably unjustly, of having been accessory to her husband's murder. As to the charge of having married Bothwell, Lord of Liddesdale, one of his murderers, she is believed to have been influenced in so doing by fear. Her infant son was placed on the throne, with her half-brother James, Earl of Murray, as Regent, [Four illegitimate brothers accompanied Mary from France, all of whom were hostile to her.] who had throughout been her secret enemy. On September 8th, 1567, an Act was passed by the Parliament summoning certain chiefs in Dumfriesshire to appear at Edinburgh, and consult on a mode of pacifying the Borders, which were much agitated in favour of the deposed Queen. "Forasmuch as on our Sovereign Lord's coronation," it ran, "and acceptation of the office of Regent of the realm by his dearest relation, James, Earl of Murray, &c., &c., he charges and ordains Patrick, Bishop of Wigton, William Gordon, Alexander Gordon, John Gordon, Maxwell, Lord Carlyle, Thomas Kirkpatrick, Charles Murray of Cockpool, and John Johnstone of that Ilk to appear in person at Edinburgh," &c. But the Queen's escape the next year set the whole Borders in a flame, and her army of nearly 600 men was chiefly collected from Galloway, Annandale, Nithsdale, and Liddesdale. Many of the Dumfriesshire chiefs signed a bond to support her cause, among them Hay, Lord Yester, Maxwell, Herries, Edward Maxwell, Abbot of Dundrennan, Crichton, and the Lairds of Ros, Seaton, Somerville, Johnstone, and Lochinvar; while Drumlanrig, Lord Home, Glencairne, Lindsay, the Earl of Morton, and many more, took the part of the Regent. The rival forces met at Langside, two miles from Glasgow, where the Queen's troops sustained a decisive defeat, May 13th, and escaping on horseback, through Crawford, Sanquhar, and Dumfries, to Dundrennan in Galloway, she adopted the fatal resolution of crossing over to England to ask for protection from Queen Elizabeth.

Three weeks later the Regent Murray followed up his victory by an armed progress through Dumfriesshire to restore order, and take an oath of allegiance from the chiefs. At Crawford, in Lanarkshire, the castle surrendered, for its owner Sir James Hamilton (Johnstone's uncle) had been captured at Langside. Sanquhar also surrendered and was spared, as Lord Crichton promised to repair to Edinburgh within a given time. Gordon of Lochinvar was more obdurate, and two of his castles were burnt down; and on the 18th of June, the Regent marched to Dumfries, and taking possession of a large house belonging to Lord Maxwell, stayed there all the next day, expecting the owner to do homage to him. Maxwell had been there the preceding morning, with the Laird of Johnstone, Maxwell of Cowhill, and Lochinvar, and a thousand of their men, and they had cleared the town of provisions; but he never presented himself to the Regent, and it was supposed that his colleagues restrained him from doing so. Several of the Maxwells, Irvings, Grahames, and Bells, came and offered their homage, and John Johnstone, the Laird of Newbie, gave a pledge for the fidelity of all the Johnstones, consequently the Regent abstained from burning the two castles of the Laird of Johnstone—Lochwood Tower and Lochouse Tower—which he occupied on his return. [Holinshed's History of Scotland. State Papers.] On June 20th, he marched to Hoddom Castle belonging to Lord Herries, near which he encountered a band of 1000 outlaws, a few of whom he captured. Hoddom yielded the next day, when the Laird of Drumlanrig was placed in it and reappointed Warden of the Marches, a post he had held since 1553. "Great hunger," writes Holinshed, "began to pinch in the army. A pint of wine was sold at seven shillings Scots, and no bread to be had for any money." Annan capitulated on being invested with 1000 men, and the Regent had an interview there with Lord Scrope, the English Warden of the Marches. Lochmaben was also taken from the Maxwells, and near Lochwood the army seized on a large quantity of cattle. On the 24th June it arrived at Peebles, and the following day at Edinburgh; but bands of outlaws still continued to harass the country under pretence of fighting for the Queen. In the Register of the Privy Council for October, 1569, a list is given of these depredators, whom their chiefs were bound over to arrest or keep in check. Under the head of Will Bell of Gretno we read "the which day John Johnstone of Gretno (or Graitney) obliges himself that Will Bell of Gretno shall be punished for disobedience of the laws." John Johnstone of Graitney also pledges himself for the good conduct of the Irvings, and the Laird of Johnstone and John Johnstone of Newbie pledged themselves for the good conduct of the gang of Fairholm.

On hearing of Queen Mary's flight to England through the assistance of Lord Herries, the Regent immediately caused him to be proclaimed an outlaw. Herries wrote from Dumfries, September, 1568, to the English Privy Council to intercede on behalf of his unhappy sovereign, and a month later went to London to try and obtain a personal interview with Elizabeth. Failing in this he visited France to plead for Queen Mary with her brother-in-law, Henry III., and encouraged by the assassination of the Regent Murray in 1569, tried to organise another military movement in her favour on his return. To put this down, and to avert an incursion of the Borderers into England, Queen Elizabeth sent an army under Lord Scrope to ravage the Border estates of those Lairds and Noblemen particularly attached to Mary's cause, and her orders were barbarously carried out.

Scrope reported from Carlisle, April 21st, 1570, that he had encamped at Ecclefechan, and sent Musgrave to burn Hoddom Maynes (i.e., Newbie Mains), Trailtrow, Ryuthwell, Calpole, Blackshaw, Sherrington, Bankend, Lochar, and Old Cockpool; that at the last place, in an encounter with Lord Maxwell, he had taken 100 prisoners, including the Alderman of Dumfries and 16 Burgesses, but had afterwards been driven back by Lords Maxwell and Carlyle, and by Charteris, Grierson, Kirkpatrick, and Carruthers. At Cummertrees he had another battle with them, when he captured several Lairds; Maxwell, Carlyle, Johnstone, and other chiefs only escaping "by the strength of the Laird of Cockpool's house, and a great wood and morass." He had been ordered to spare Douglas of Drumlanrig's tenants, but they opposed him as fiercely as the rest. Another of Scrope's lieutenants, Lord Sussex, wrote to the Secretary, Cecil, that he had thrown down the Castle at Annan, and had not left a stone house standing in that town, which was an "ill neighbour to Carlisle." The insurgents are described by Buchanan as Highlanders and Borderers, the Laird of Fairniherst, the Johnstones and Armstrongs, the Grants and the Clan Chattan, besides the Maxwells; but Drumlanrig and his son-in-law, Jardine of Applegirth, remained attached to the young King. He accuses the Borderers of "misorder and cruelty, not only usit in war, but detestable to all barbarous and wild Tartars, in slaying of prisoners, and contrary to all humanity and justice, keeping no promise to miserable captives." After the whole of Scotland had been agitated for more than two years, and pestilene had broken out, the insurrection was finally suppressed, and the English retired from Dumfriesshire.

As before stated, the Lairds of Teviotdale signed a bond at Kelso, under the auspices of Scot of Buccleuch, in 1169, to support the infant King James VI. against the Queen's adherents in Dumfriesshire. Consequently they escaped the English ravages. James Gledstanes of Cocklaw was one of those who signed it; and Gladstane of Gladstane, took part in the skirmish called the Raid of Redswire in 1575 under a Scot. Though the headquarters of this family were in Lanarkshire and Peebles, they are early found in Dumfriesshire, and Herbert de Gledstanes of that county signed the Ragman's roll in 1296. In 1455 Herbert de Gledstanes of that Ilk and Homer de Gledstanes were deputy-sheriffs of Dumfriesshire under Lord Maxwell, the Warden of the borders, and from the uncommon name of Homer being found at that time in the Maxwell family there may have been some family connection between the Maxwells and Gledstanes. In 1517 and in 1543 Herbert Gledstanes was one of the bailies of the town of Dumfries. In 1579 William Gledstanes, son of this Herbert, was a bailie, and the records of Dumfries show that he had two brothers also burgesses of the same town, viz., John and James Gledstanes, the first of whom was returned heir to their father in 1564. Herbert, probably another brother, is mentioned in connection with Dumfries in 1572, but was a bailile of Kirkcudbright at that date. The familiar name of Catherine Gledstanes is also found in the burgh books of that period, as the wife of Adam Paterson and Walter Gledstanes of Craggis appears in the Dumfries burgh books of 1575. James Gledstanes left an only daughter, who married Robert Mackynell, but his brother left sons, and a Herbert Gledstanes appears again among the bailies of Dumfries in 1622. Sir James Gledstanes is mentioned in 1578. He was probably in Holy Orders, as the term Sir was generally applied to priests.

The old bard, Scot of Satchells, describes the establishment of his chief, Scot of Buccleuch, at Branxholm in the early part of the 17th century. Possibly he enlarged as much on facts as Sir Walter Scott has done on his description—

No baron was better served in Britain;
The barons of Buckleugh they kept their call,
Four and twenty gentlemen in their hall,
All being of his name and kin;
Each two had a servant to wait upon them.

But he explains in prose that although 23 of these gentlemen bore the name of Scot, the other was Walter Gledstanes, a near cousin of my lord's.

As late as 1619, there is an action brought against James Johnstone, brother's son to the Laird of Westraw (ancestor to Sir Frederick Johnstone), for having robbed his master, in which he is described as household man and servitor to Irving of Wisbie. It was thought no degradation for the younger sons of a laird's family to act as serving men in another house. The mercantile class in Scotland was chiefly drawn from that source, for the prejudice against entering into trade which we still find among the landed gentry in Germany and some other countries never seems to have existed here. The will of John Johnstone, merchant, brother to the late James Johnstone, Laird of Westraw, is proved on June 4, 1576, and several of the Johnstones of Newbie and of that Ilk, of the Maxwells, Kirkpatricks, and other Dumfriesshire families were merchants. A relationship with a provincial chief was extremely useful in early days, as it ensured a safe conduct through any district in which his authority was respected; and the merchant living in a town, probably a seaport, and with more education than his country cousin, was a very useful relative for a laird to possess. The Gladstones therefore followed the prevalent custom when their junior branches migrated into towns and set up in business, as they grew too numerous for the hereditary land to support.

The names of all the men in the burgh of Annan, on September 9, 1591, are given in a bond of man-rent with Lord Maxwell. When the Annandale Peerage claims were last heard, an advocate pleaded that Johnstone was at that date the commonest name in Annandale among all classes. But in this list of nearly 100 names only two Johnstones appear, and both of them connected with the Newbie family, and in all the deeds I have collected at that period whatever Johnstones are named were related in a left-handed way or otherwise to the chiefs of the house. These men of Annan were Littles, Tods, Wilkins, Hairs, Irvings, Veilds, Halidays, Louche (probably Losh, still a Cumberland name, or Loch, for in 1603 Robert Loch was a bailie of Annan, and collector of His Majesty's revenues), Wilsons, Raes, Vauche (Welsh?), Menzies, Rigs, Blacks, Richardsons, Potts, Galloways, Carliles, Millars, Bournans, Gasks, Hutchins, Palmers, Bells, Whites, Tyndings, Robesons, Grahams, Smyths, Warriors, Corbets, Mikes, Hegis, and two John Johnstones. David Millar was notary public.

Chapter Eight

Sir James Douglas of Drumlanrig, who succeeded Lord Herries as Warden of the Borders in 1553, retained it and his allegiance to the Ministry in power till his death in 1578, notwithstanding a near relationship to Lord Maxwell and Gordon of Lochinvar, and a family connection with the other leading insurgents. In 1564 he obtained a charter of the Barony of Mouswald from marriage or exchange with one of the heiresses of Simon Carruthers. His eldest daughter was married to Charteris of Amisfield, a second to Edward, Lord Crichton of Sanquhar, a third to Grierson of Lag, a fourth to James Tweedie of Drumelzier, a fifth to Alexander Stewart of Garlies, and a sixth to

John Jardine of Applegirth; and his son William married to his cousin, the daughter of Lochinvar. At this period nearly all the chief families were related to each other. The eldest son of Lord Maxwell [The superiority of Maxwell to the other Border chiefs is shown by a deed in which he asked the pardon of Robert Dalziell for having killed his father.] (who died in 1546), like his father, had been a prisoner in England. He did not survive his release many years, but having married Lady Beatrice Douglas, left a posthumous son, Robert, to inherit his honours in 1552, under the guardianship of Lord Herries, often called the master of Maxwell, being the heir-presumptive to the title.

The old Laird of Johnstone died Nov. 8, 1567, leaving a grandson, John, who the next year was engaged at Langside on the part of the Queen. His daughters were married to John Maitland of Auchencastle, to Adam Grahame, to a Carruthers of Mouswald, and to Christopher Irving of Bonshaw (a valiant soldier, who had been a prisoner in the hands of the English), and his granddaughter Janet was married to the eldest son of Lord Carlyle. His will, [A codicil to this will was the subject of a long lawsuit by his heir against his widow and youngest son. Nicholas Douglas, the widow, pleaded that he was a very old man, and could no longer write, so she had signed it for him.] made in 1562, left Lord Herries joint executor with his widow, and also desired his heir to be guided by the counsels of Lord Herries and the Lairds of Drumlanrig and Elphinstone. He bequeathed his horse, hart, sword, and dogs to Lord Herries. His younger son John was imprisoned in Edinburgh Castle in 1564, at "the instance of John Douglas of Raecleuch, for not desisting and ceasing from the lands of Raecleuch," but was released on bail a few months afterwards, his securities being John Johnstone, commendator of Salsit, and James Johnstone, burgess of Edinburgh.

Adam Johnstone of Corry, another brother, was dead in October, 1544, leaving a son, James. William Johnstone of Newbie and Graitney was dead in 1565. His eldest legitimate son John, Baron of Newbie, married Marion Carruthers, and another son became Laird of Cummertrees. William, heir of Newbie, married a relation of Lord Maxwell, the daughter of John Maxwell of Brackenside or of Hills, and died before his father, leaving a young son, John. In 1574 a dispute had arisen between several of the Laird of Johnstone's followers and the young Lord Maxwell, which extended to both chiefs, for both aspired to the Wardenry of the West Marches, which Sir James Douglas of Drumlanrig had virtually resigned from age and infirmity, though no other was appointed till after his death. The Earl of Morton, also a Douglas, who became Regent in 1572, desired the two families to refer their difficulties to the Lords in Council, and the Laird of Johnstone and Lord Maxwell each appointed certain noblemen and friends to represent them in Edinburgh, any four, three, or two on each side being empowered to act for all. Maxwell selected his own relations and kinsmen. Johnstone also nominated relations and connections—John Johnstone of Newbie, the Earl of Rothes, Sir James Balfour, Sir James Hamilton, William Livingstone of Jerviswood, Thomas Johnstone of Craighopburne, Robert Douglas of Cassehogil, Walter Scott of Guildlands, and

Walter Scot of Tuschelaw. The deputies were to meet at Edinburgh on the next Feb. 15th, both parties promising to keep good rule in the country during their absence. John Johnstone of Newbie died in Edinburgh, Feb. 1577; but the dispute seems to have been settled to the advantage of his chief, who, the following year was made Warden of the Borders and knighted, an honour enjoyed by some of his ancestors. He also came forward as a candidate, though unsuccessfully, for the office of Provost of Dumfries, which had hitherto been held by the members or friends of the Maxwell family. His audacity in contesting it gave additional displeasure to Lord Maxwell, who prevented him and his followers from entering the town with an armed force. A family feud of old standing was revived, till Maxwell having quarrelled with the King's favourite (Lord Arran) was declared an outlaw by James VI., on the ground that he protected the robber Armstrongs. Johnstone, in his capacity of Warden, was ordered to pursue and arrest him, and two bands of soldiers under William Baillie of Lamington and Captain Cranstown were sent to assist him. The soldiers were defeated at Crawfordmuir by Maxwell's half-brother Robert, and as the Johnstones were a much smaller clan than Lord Maxwell's, whose cadets were now established in all parts of Dumfriesshire, they were also dispersed, and Lochwood Tower besieged and burned; Robert Maxwell observing as he

watched the flames that he would give Lady Johnstone light to set her hood. Among other losses the ancient family deeds were destroyed. Johnstone again attacked his rival, but was taken prisoner, and though released in little more than a year, when a compromise was made by the King with his rebel subject, he

Spedlings

died very soon afterwards—it is said from shame and grief at his defeat— 1586. Maxwell, with Scot of Buccleuch and a company of Nithsdale men, besides Beatties, Littles, and Armstrongs, and 340 from Lower Annandale, marched upon Stirling, and effected their purpose of deposing the favourite Arran, who was deprived of his title and estates, and of obtaining from the Parliament a full amnesty for themselves and their allies. Those from Lower Annandale consisted of Bells, Carrutherses, and Irvings, and a troop of cavalry furnished by George Carruthers of Holmains and Charles Carruthers, his son.

The tenants of the Newbie, Graitney, and Cummertrees estates, of course, followed their chief.

After the death of Johnstone, Maxwell was appointed Warden of the Marches, and formed a bond of affiance with the young James, Laird of Johnstone, when he married Sarah Maxwell, the granddaughter of the celebrated Lord Herries, who had died in 1582. One of Johnstone's sisters was also married to Sir Robert Maxwell of Orchardstone; so that for some years there was peace between the two families. The young Laird of Newbie was married to a daughter of Sir Alexander Stewart of Garlies (son-in-law to Douglas of Drumlanrig, the late Warden of the Marches), and lived chiefly in Edinburgh; but five of his uncles represented the Newbie Johnstones in Dumfriessshire.

The will of his grandfather, John, Laird of Newbie, shows the extent of their lands. "The Testament and inventory of the gudes, geir, soumes of money, and debts pertaining to the late John Johnstone of Newby, within the Sheriffdom of Dumfries the time of his decease, who died on the 10th day of February, the year of God, 1577, faithfully made and given up by Marioun Carruthers, his relict, whom he nominated his only executor in his latter will underwritten of the date, at the lodging of the late Mr James Lyndsay, within the burgh of Edinburgh, upon the 5th and 6th days of February, 1577, beforesaid, before these witnesses—Robert Johnstone in Cummertrees, John Johnstone oy (grandson) and apparent heir to the Laird of Holmendes, John Brown of the Land, and John Johnstone, writer in Edinburgh, and divers others. . . . The said John Johnstone of Newby being sick in body, but whole in mind, submits himself soul and body to the mercy of God, recommending his wife and bairnes to the favour, protection, and maintenance of the Regent's grace and the Earl of Angus, Lieutenant and Warden of the West Marches, which he is persuaded they shall find for the good and true service that he has made, and always intended to make, under the King's majesty for ever if it had been God's pleasure longer to continue his days, beseeching the said Earl of Angus that by his lordship's means it may please the Regent's grace to dispone the ward and marriage of the said John, grandson to the said Marioun Carruthers, his wife, for the help of his four younger sons. He makes and constitutes the said Marioun Carruthers, his wife, so continuing in her pure widowhood, tutrix testamentor to his grandson and apparent heir. He makes Robert Johnstone, his son, his assignee to his right possession and kindness of his lands in the town of Annan, except such as is annexed and possessed with the Mains of Newbie, and wills the said Robert to be good and friendly to the poor men of Annan, occupiers of the same land. He leaves to the said Robert his right possession and kindness to the kirk and tithes of Kirkpatrick-Fleming, and also makes him assignee to his lease to run of the lands of — within the lordship of Dundrennan, recommending the said Robert to the favour, protection, and maintenance of my Lord Herries, beseeching his lordship not only to extend the same to the said Robert, accepting him in his lordship's service and continuing him in the lease and possession of that land for his service, and also to stand good lord to his wife and remaining bairns. To his son John he leaves his

house in Dumfries and money; to his brother, John Johnstone of Cummertrees, a portion of his lands of Ryehill, and the remaining portion to his son
Edward; to his fifth son, Abraham, he leaves lands in Middlebie, and to his son
William lands in Stapleton. To his youngest son David he leaves lands in Robgill, and also the lease of certain lands which had been settled upon his widowed daughter-in-law and her husband on their marriage, the said David paying to her thankfully the duty contained in the said lease during her lifetime."

In 1582 Robert Johnstone received a grant of the lands of Northfield and
Brigholme, near Annan, from the King, "who followed the good example of his
noble ancestors," so the charter runs, "in rewarding useful lieges, and solici-
tous for good and honest holders of the royal lands," hereby infefted "the son
of the late John Johnstone of Newbie" in lands joining his nephew's property
of Newbie and Stapleton and his own inheritance; one of his neighbours, as
the charter also states, being Christopher Irving, or "Black Christie," on the
land of Galabank, this Christopher being son-in-law to the late Laird of Johnstone.

The Lairds of the West Marches able to keep order on the Borders in 1587
are given in the 95th Act of the 11th Parliament of James VI.—"Lord Maxwell;
Douglas, Laird of Drumlanrig; the Laird of Johnstone; Jardine, Laird of Applegirth; Carruthers, Laird of Holmains; Johnstone, Laird of Graitney; Maxwell,
Lord Herries; the Laird of Dunwidie (an estate lying between Wamphray, Corrie, and Kirkpatrick-Fleming), and Gordon, Laird of Lochinvar." The same
were appointed Constables on the Borders in 1597, and also Johnstone of
Newbie. A grandson of James Johnstone of Wamphray brought about a seri-
ous civil feud. He was known as the Galliard (a gay, reckless character), and in
1593 was seized by some of the Crichtons while carrying off one of their
horses, and he was hung before his nephew William's eyes in spite of the
younger Johnstone's offers and entreaties. This led to a skirmish, when, according to the ballad of "The Lads of Wamphray," "the Biddes burn three days
ran blood," and the Crichtons, who suffered the most, appealed for redress to
the Warden, Lord Maxwell; while fifteen widows whose husbands had fallen
in the fight went to Edinburgh to lodge a petition with the King and his council, and caused a great sensation by marching through the streets carrying the
dead men's blood-stained clothes. The Laird of Johnstone was summoned to
Edinburgh to answer the charge, and was imprisoned in the Castle, but escaped on the 4th of June, 1593, and returned to Dumfriesshire to collect his
followers. He was proclaimed an outlaw, and Maxwell ordered to arrest him;
but before attempting it the Warden formed a secret bond of manrent with
Douglas of Drumlanrig, Crichton, Kirkpatrick of Closeburn, and others who
agreed to support him. He had signed an agreement with Johnstone only the
previous year, in which they had obliged themselves to "freely remit and forgive all rancours of mind, grudge, malice, and feuds that had passed or fallen
between them in any time bygone." The new agreement was, according to
Spottiswood, "kept so carelessly that it fell into the hands of Johnstone of
Cummertrees," not a vassal of Maxwell's, as is sometimes stated, and he gave

it up to his chief, who on receiving Maxwell's formal summons to surrender for trial scornfully cast it aside and prepared for battle. Maxwell was assisted by some of the royal troops, and assembled two thousand men under his banner at Lochmaben; but Johnstone, assisted by his mother's relations, the Scots of Eskdale and Teviotdale, the Elliots of Liddesdale, and the divisions of his own clan, who counted among their retainers the Bells, Irvings, and Grahames of Graitney, brought more than half that number to Dryfesdale, where, near a farm and moor called Torwood, the battle of Dryfe Sands was fought. The young Laird of Newbie seems to have abstained from taking a personal part in the battle, his maternal grandfather, Maxwell of Brackenside, being on the opposite side with eighty followers, as well as his wife's relations, but his uncle, Robert Johnstone, was there, two Johnstones of Cummertrees (one of whom was killed), as well as the Johnstones of Graitney, with the Newbie and Graitney tenants. The Johnstones were entrenched in a good position when Maxwell's army crossed the Annan to attack them, but it is said that they disdained to take this advantage of the enemy, and came down into the open plain, where, owing to the skill with which he handled his men, Sir James Johnstone (for he had been knighted) gained a complete victory. Before the battle Maxwell had offered a ten pound land to the soldier who should bring him Johnstone's head or hand. Hearing of this, Sir James declared that he had not a ten pound land to give, but he would reward any man with a five merk land who should bring him Maxwell's head or hand and the prize was gained by William Johnstone of Wamphray (the nephew of the Galliard), who pursued him as he was flying, and struck off the hand which he stretched out for quarter, while Douglas, Kirkpatrick, and Grierson escaped by the fleetness of their horses. A story is some times told that Maxwell finally perished by the hand of a daughter of that Laird of Johnstone, who had been his prisoner, and who had died in consequence of shame and grief, but this is generally discredited. Another story states that this female fiend was the wife of James Johnstone of Kirkton, [Sir Archibald Johnstone (he spelt it Johnstown) of Warriestoun executed in 1663 for his share in the Revolution, was son of James Johnstone of Beirholme, who, in 1608, was returned heir to his grand father, Gavine Johnstone of Kirkton in Kirkpatrick-Juxta. They came of the Elsieschellis family. The Johnstones of Castlemilk migrated about 1620 from Dumfriesshire to the east borders, where they founded a family, being previously of Kellobank, a branch of the Johnstones of Elsieschellis who are found in the 15th century. The old poet-laureate Rare Ben Jonson, imagined that his ancestors came from Annandale, but there is no proof of it, and I cannot find the name Benjamin in any branch of the Johnstones. Born in 1574, the son of a clergyman, he was educated at Westminster School, and ran away from home to serve as a soldier in the Netherlands to escape being employed as a builder, which was his step-father's trade. At one period of career, as an actor and poet, he did undertake a tour on foot to Annandale with the hope of finding relations there, but we do not hear that he succeeded, and Jonson is a very old English name. It is distinguished from the Scottish Johnestoune as early as

Edward I.] who lived not far from the field, and had come to seek her husband among the wounded, when Maxwell lying fainting under a tree appealed to her compassion, William of Wamphray having abstained from putting him to death, as he was the King's lieutenant. At any rate, Maxwell, a brave and well educated nobleman, was killed in carrying out the King's express command, and Sir James Johnstone and his companions were at once outlawed, "no man daring," as a contemporary diarist states, "to take any of them into his house."

It was a curious result of the battle of Dryfe Sands that, little more than two years after Sir James Johnstone had defied the King's lieutenant and caused his death, he should have been invested with his victim's office of Warden of the Marches; but the Scottish Cabinet had conceived a great dread of the power of England during Elizabeth's reign, and avoided nothing more than a breach of their present harmony. For this it was essential that the outlaws on the Border should be kept from troubling their formidable neighbour, and the Laird, under whose banner they had lately fought, was the most likely to be able to do it. So much were they feared that a law passed in 1587 prevented any Border man from even entering Fife, Peebles, or Lothian without a pledge, in consequence of an application to the convention of Royal Burghs from the town of Peebles, June 4, 1583. "The same day a complaint was given in anent the great injuries done to them by the four clans of Johnstone, Grahames, Elliots, and Armstrongs, and what redress may be reasonablest obtained thereof." Perhaps the King also remembered that the death of Johnstone's father was caused by a similar defiance of his delegated authority on the part of Maxwell, the King having prevented a reconciliation between the rival chiefs. A letter from the Master of Gray to Johnstone, dated Stirling, September 4, 1585, informs him "of a report having reached His Majesty and the Court that all the Johnstones had appointed with Maxwell." "The King," he says, "disbelieves it, but desires to be advertised with certainty." William Johnstone, one of the original students of the University of Edinburgh, where he graduated in 1587, was presented by James VI. to the living of Lockerbie about 1592. He requested the Presbytery to give him an exchange, as he "durst not repair to Dumfriesshire on account of the feud between the Maxwells and the Johnstones," but his petition was not attended to; and he was killed in the street of Lockerbie in 1595, being only 29 years of age, merely because of his name. Those members of the Maxwell, Johnstone, Douglas, and Scot families of an unwarlike disposition had no resource but to leave Dumfriesshire; and several went to Edinburgh, where they became merchants, and were often much richer than the chiefs of their clans. A warrant was obtained by Sir James Johnstone in 1594, under the King's sign manual, directing the Privy Council to grant a respite for five years, Dec. 24, in favour of Sir James and eight score followers, for the pursuit and slaughter of John Lord Maxwell, His Majesty's lieutenant and Warder for the time, and of sundry other his Majesty's subjects who were in company with him, the ruining and burning of the Kirk of Lochmaben, and the slaughter of Captain Oliphant and others. The names of those respited are given in the following order:—"Sir James Johnstone of

Dunskellie, John Carmichael, Robert Johnstone of Raycleuch (who was only eleven years old), Symon Johnston, (half) brother to the Laird of Johnstone, Robert Johnstone in Brigholme (of Newby), William Johnstone, younger of Graitney, John Johnstone in Cummertrees, William Johnstone of Elsiechellis, Adam, his brother, and many other Johnstones, including those of Kirkhill, besides Irvings, Moffats, Carrutherses, Scots, Elliots, Stewarts, Chisholm, Grahame, Armstrong, and Murrays." Lord Herries, who immediately succeeded Maxwell as Warden, paid little attention to this respite, although he was Johnstone's brother-in-law, but tried to pursue and punish some of Johnstone's followers, till he kept the country in such a state of confusion that the King ended in superseding him by Johnstone himself. The Johnstones were certainly regarded with more favour by Lord Scrope and the English Cabinet than the Maxwell family, who were supposed to be attached to France. There is a letter preserved in the English Record Office from Sir James Johnstone to the Earl of Bothwell, 1592, promising "upon his faith, honour, and truth to support whatever he shall promise to the Queen of England concerning the forthsetting of religion, the surety of the King, and the preservation of the amity with England." Another letter from the English Ambassador to Cecil, [Queen Elizabeth's Secretary, and ancestor to Lord Salisbury.] in 1599, recommending Edward Johnstone (one of the Newbie family), a merchant in Edinburgh, who was going to the Low countries, and offered to do service there for the English, states that Edward Johnstone is very "inward"— i.e., intimate—with his chief, who is one of the "most honest men in these parts."

With the appointment of Johnstone as Warden of the Middle Marches, and his relation Scot of Buccleuch as Warden of the East Marches, the Border disturbances seem to have been compressed into personal quarrels between the chiefs. Maxwell married Hamilton's daughter, and this powerful Laird (as well as Douglas of Drumlanrig) could not forgive their defeat at Dryfe Sands. On July 13th, 1597, there was a fight between the Laird of Drumlanrig and Johnstone, and "their assisters," and shortly afterwards Johnstone was again deprived of the Wardenry, but it was given to his ally, Sir John Carmichael. Birrell, the Edinburgh diarist, writes, May 27th, 1598—"The Laird of Johnstone's picture was hung at the (market) cross of Edinburgh with his head downwards, and declared a mansworn man, and upon June 5 he and his accomplices were put to the born and pronounced rebels at the cross by open proclamation." This appears to have been in consequence of Johnstone having failed to seize "John and Jock Armstrong and others," as he had been directed by the Privy Council, June 29, 1597; so his enemies accused him of collusion with them. A letter from the English Ambassador to Cecil, Oct. 12, 1599, alludes to this faction against Johnstone. "On Tuesday last the Council going to the King to Linlithgow for resolution about the Border causes, the Earl of Angus, the Lord Hamilton, and sundry others being there in Johnstone's contrary, and the Lord of Buccleuch and others there in his favour, the matter was hardly reasoned that day and the next day forenoon, Angus (for now the cause is his against the Lord of Johnstone) alleging he could get no sufficient pledges of the Johnstones; and Johnstone that sufficient pledges were offered him, and needlessly and wrongfully he raised these troubles in Annandale. But the trial thereof is continued till Tuesday se'ennight, and George Murray, one of the King's chamber, sent to receive Lochmaben Castle for the King, Johnstone being directed to write with him to that effect. This George Murray is Johnstone's own. In all appearance the day of trial and confronting the lieutenant and Johnstone will be exceeding great, and may well breed a great stir, which I verily look far. In the meantime Angus is not to meddle with the Johnstones." On November 12th, 1599, the Ambassador writes again. "On Thursday the Laird of Johnstone brought in most of his pledges, and is gone to bring the rest of Thursday next, and thereafter to be freed and go hence; the Laird of Buccleuch staying only to see him at good peace hath brought the matter between him and Sanquhar and Drumlanrig to end in effect, Johnstone having subscribed an assurance, and they two to do the like, or the King to strait them, but they have promised the King to subscribe; the Laird of Buccleuch hereon hath taken leave of the King and Queen and gone by sea."

"The Lord-lieutenant Angus came not with his pledges, but excused the same, and is to bring them this week; the country they mean thus to quiet, and that Carmichael shall be Warden, and Johnstone to assist him."

Johnstone's "assurance," above mentioned, is signed by himself and by his pledges, John Johnstone of Graitney and Gilbert Johnstone of Wamphray. On July 2, 1600, he was solemnly acquitted, and "restored to his honours," writes Birrell, at the cross of Edinburgh by the proclamation of a herald and four trumpets. The same year he was again made Warden, Carmichael having been murdered by some of the Armstrongs as he was going to open a court at Lochmaben. [In 1602, James Johnstone of Westraw pledged himself for William Irving, the younger of Kirkton, and Robert Carlile of Bridekirk, while Sir James Johnstone of Dunskellie guaranteed James Carlile of Soupilbank. The heirs of the Carliles of Bridekirk possess the monument of their ancestor who was buried in Annan Churchyard. On it he is called Herbert, yet the printed Acta Dom.Con, always call him Robert. He married Margaret Cunningham. "Heir lyes the body of a worthy gentleman Herbert Carliell, Laird of Brydekirk, who lived in credit and commendation among his friends, and died in Christ Sept. 1632, of his age 74." The arms are below.]

On March 14th, 1600, Nicolson writes to Cecil that "Johnstone has twice stayed the Armstrongs very honestly," and that he begins "to smell" that he has been put in fear of Borders breaking by device. In another letter he alludes to the anxiety felt for James VI. to succeed Queen Elizabeth on the English throne, as it was thought that otherwise Scotland would be certainly annexed to England by conquest. The Scots, he said, were greatly disheartened by their losses in the last war with England.

An uncle of Sir John Carmichael had entered the service of Muscovy, and assisted the Czar, Ivan the Terrible, in 1569 to subdue the rebellious towns of Novogorod and Pleskof. He was made Governor of Pleskof.

Since the reformed Catholic religion was established in Scotland in 1560 the alliance with France had been much weakened. It was clear to the Scottish leaders that their country could not long continue to maintain its independence, and if it were to be annexed by one or the other, of course the reformers preferred England, who was doing them good service by keeping their unhappy Queen in prison. In the French archives a deed is preserved, dated April 14 (Easter Eve), at Fontainebleau, evidently obtained from the youthful Mary under pressure from her future father-in-law, Henry II., and her other relatives. It is endorsed in French. "Act by which the Queen of Scots, considering the great expenses made by the late King, Francis I., and by the reigning King, Henry II., to protect the Kingdom of Scotland against the English, and after having taken counsel of her best and special friends, the Rev, and Illustrious Cardinal Lorraine and M. le Duc de Guize, her uncles, declares, wills, and ordains that, in default of heirs of her body, the King of France, who is or will be, shall have and enjoy the Kingdom of Scotland, its revenues, &c., till the payment of a million of gold for the cost of maintaining the kingdom." Just a year later Mary was married to the Dauphin, afterwards Francis II., who died in 1559.

The subsequent rigour of the Scottish Government against Roman priests, who were liable to execution if found in Scotland, while any accused of attending their ministrations, or of even professing Romanism, were exiled, is explained by the constant intrigues carried on by the Pope and his allies in France and Spain against Elizabeth and James for the sake of re-establishing the Roman supremacy where it had been lost, and as a faithful daughter of the Roman Church, Mary could hardly avoid sharing in them. It is easy to imagine the horror with which the news of the suppression of the monastries, the confiscation of Church property, the execution of the abbots and priests who refused to acknowledge Henry. VIII. instead of the Pope as the head of the Church, and the prohibition of the Mass was received by devout Churchmen on the continent.

The reign of Mary I. in England had been long enough to restore a large portion of its confiscated property to the Church, so the State could no longer be pointed out as the recipient of stolen goods; but Rome had not the distribution of them, and the Pope saw that Elizabeth's comparative tolerance was more fatal to his cause than the avaricious ferocity of the King, whom his predecessor had styled the Defender of the Faith.

In 1586 Robert Bruce, a Scotsman, wrote to invite Philip II. of Spain to occupy Scotland, and "in this way bring back, the Catholic faith in the end also to England and Ireland; for in Scotland heresy would be destroyed at its root, the English would be expelled from the low countries, and France would thus obtain the key to their kingdom."

The agitation on the Scottish Borders was undoubtedly sustained by the imprisoned Queen's emissaries, but at last, in November, 1587, her fate was sealed. On the 23d she wrote to the Spanish Ambassador in England after her condemnation thanking him "for the last time" for the interest he had taken in her captivity, and esteeming herself "happy to die for the Catholic religion, though her enemies say that she is dying for having wished to murder the Queen." A general mourning was ordered throughout Scotland, and it was openly said that nothing but war could wash off the blot from Scotland's shield. This feeling was so strong on the Borders that in addition to the irritation caused by the Reformation, there was a pretext for constant bickering where the English and Scots came so closely in contact. A letter is preserved with the signature in cipher addressed from Greenwich to a counsellor of James VI, March, 1588. It seeks to prove to him that "the King of Scotland ought not to undertake to avenge the death of his mother, but, on the contrary, to do everything possible to bring about the union of the two crowns, for if for that occasion he tries to make war against this kingdom, he must consider two points—first, if the war would appear just and honest in the sight of any one, and of the means of persevering in it, and what would be the conclusion and end; and secondly, that his pretensions to the succession might fall in the struggle." The author of the letter, after a long dissertation on each of these points, concludes that the end of the war would be the ruin of Scotland, and begs the King not to attempt it.

Another letter of 1597 from Queen Elizabeth to James VI., preserved in the London Record Office, contains a sharp rebuke; the King having opened his Parliament with a speech in which he complained of the wrong done him in the death of his mother, holding back his annuity, and efforts to deprive him of his title to the Crown of England. "When the strange blast of flying fame," she writes, "first pierced her ears she thought that it had brought report of some untruth, but when the records of his Parliament were witness of his pronounced words she wondered what evil spirits had possessed him to set forth such infamous devices void of any show of truth. She is sorry that he is so fallen, and will need throw himself into such a hurpoole of bottomless credit. She never yet loved him so little as not to moan his infamous dealings, but he must be assured that he deals with such a King as will bear no wrongs, nor endure infamy, and that without large amends she may not and will not slupper up such indignities." This letter produced an apology from King James, but it shows that he was not quite so indifferent to the fate of his mother as was affirmed by Queen Elizabeth's enemies, who had hoped that he would cast off the English alliance and the Reformed faith as soon as he came of age. The Spanish Ambassador, writing to the King of Spain in 1587, thinks that James had a secret preference for the Roman faith. "The King of Scotland," he writes, "arrived on the 12th of April at Dumfries to put his hand on Maxwell's collar." But the last, who was the prop of the Roman faith in Dumfriesshire, "had gone the preceding night, being warned by the great lords." He suspects it to have been by order of the King himself.

When the Roman priests were dismissed from the country no one took their place in some instances for thirty or forty years, and even more, on the Borders. Early in the 17th century James VI. issued a proclamation to appoint clergy throughout Annandale. "The inhabitants thereof," says this document, "are for the most part wild heathen men," and for at least a generation they had no chance of being anything else. John Johnstone of Newbie, from his will in 1578, seems to have outwardly embraced the Reformed opinions, like his chief; but his grandson was outlawed in 1593 and 1602 for hearing Mass, and having his children baptized by Roman priests; and in 1595 the Laird of John-stone, Robert Johnstone of Newbie, and Charles Murray of Cockpool were charged with the same, and for entertaining Roman Catholic priests. The Church lands had been sold to laymen, and the monastic estates distributed among the King's favourites. Graitney had been for years without divine ser-vice, till Murray obtained a charter of the Barony of Dundrennan, and it was stipulated that he should pay the parson of Graitney an income of 400 marks. The zeal or half-heartedness with which the Border chiefs threw off Roman-ism had undoubtedly much to do with their success at that time; and while the Buccleuchs, Griersons, Douglases, Murrays, and some others, who were staunch Protestants, received honours and lands, the Johnstones of Newbie and Graitney, and a few more who were secretly Romanists were spoiled.

It is often forgotten that Presbyterianism did not immediately succeed Ro-manism, but that the Episcopal Church remained in Scotland for nearly a cen-tury simply divested of certain Romish principles. So late as 1649 Acts of Par-liament were passed forbidding the use of meat in Lent. The Courts of Justice were generally held on Sunday morning, showing a laxity which perhaps ac-counts for the reaction in that respect when the second Reformation was es-tablished. [Speed (temp. James Vi.) describes the Scottish gentry and nobility as very studious of learning, for which end they not only frequent the Univer-sities, but also much addict themselves to travel in foreign countries.]

The want of money in Scotland, and the love of war and adventure which characterised her hardy sons, induced many of the younger members of the Scottish families to take service in the armies on the Continent, particularly during the reign of Oliver Cromwell and after the accession of William III., when political reasons deterred some of them from accepting a commission under the Princes whom they considered to be usurpers. To be a Scotsman was undoubtedly a drawback to promotion in England till the reign of George III. or later, and the British army was very small compared to what it is now, and a commission and outfit more expensive than in a foreign force. A journey by land to London cost more than from Leith to Holland or Bremen by sea. But the sons of Scottish ministers till far into the present century crowded into the ranks of the Scottish regiments, and were distinguished for their courage and steadiness. There was not space in Scotland for the number of educated men who annually left the colleges in search of employment, so the list of the pioneers in India, America, and the West Indies is filled with Scot-tish names, and every army on the Continent, including the Turkish, con-tained officers of Scottish birth. One instance was Patrick Gordon, who en-tered the Swedish army under the grandfather of Charles XII. In a war with Poland he was captured by the enemy, and as the Poles in the days seldom exchanged prisoners, he took service with the King of Poland, who was then at war with Russia. He was impressed with the miserable condition of some Russian prisoners of war in a dungeon in Warsaw, and did his best to keep them from starvation; and in a subsequent battle with the Czar Alexis of Muscovy (father to Peter the Great), when he fell into the hands of the Russians, the Czar sent for him to thank him for having, as he had heard, "been kind to his poor subjects in Warsaw," Thereupon Gordon offered his sword to Muscovy. He and his son, and another Scotsman named Bruce, assisted the Russian armies throughout the reign of Peter the Great, and the younger Gordon published by far the best work on the reign of that monarch.

Admiral Gordon, in the service of Catherine I., was employed by Prince James, the old Chevalier, as the English Jacobite envoy at the Russian Court. Christopher Carlile, one of the Cumberland Newbie branch, commanded the Russian navy when Carmichael was governor of Pleskof, under Ivan the Terrible. He had married a daughter of Sir Francis Walsingham, and, as befitted the descendant of crusaders, he wrote a book against the commercial treaty which was formed between the Turks and England at that period. He pointed out the great risks that the traders incurred from the piratical Barbary States, on the north of Africa, and that it cost them £2000 a year in presents alone to secure even partial safe These pirates, he added, were equally dreaded by our Italian traders, and our sailors were forced to pay enormous ransoms to the Algerians for their rescue from slavery. Many petitions appear at that time, and later, among the Scottish records from prisoners captured by the Turks and Moors for assistance in paying their ransoms. One as sent from Algiers by Alexander Sanders, George Anderson, and Andrew Monro. They state that, they cannot repeat to Christian ears all the horrors they have suffered, and the scenes they daily witnessed while held in chains, the Lords in Council directed that an offertory should be made in the churches on their behalf.

In Monypeny's Chronicle, published in 1587, sixty-five lairds and gentlemen are enumerated as residing in Dumfriesshire, and the Stewartry of Kirkcudbright. Nine were Johnstones, viz., the Lairds of Johnstone, of Newbie, of Graitney, of Wamphray, [Wamphray is described in an act and decreet, 1611, as a "gentleman of very mean rent—nothing like a great baron," and his brothers "but young gentlemen without any rent or means of living."] of Corrie, of Corhead, of Craighopburne, of Newtone, and of Kirkton. Six were Gordons, viz., Lochinvar, Traquhair, Barskeoche, Airdis, Skernaes, and of the Cule. Murray of Broghton; Glendyning of Portoun; Maclellan of Bomby, and of Mertoun; Dalbeattie; Lindsay of Barcloy; Lidderdaill of St. Mary's Isle; Herries of Madinhoip, and Herries of Mabie; eight were Maxwells; Rorison [The Rorisons were M'Rories, Lords of Bute, which devolved on a son of Robert II. when the old family were deposed.] of Bardannoch; four Douglases; Macnaught of Kilquhanatie; Stewart of Fintillouche; Livingston of Little Ardie; Macnaught of that Ilk; two Crichtons; Menzies of Castlehill, and of Auchensell; Maitland of Auchencastle; Kirkpatrick of Closeburne; Kirkmichael; Grier of Lag; Charteris of Amisfield; Broune of the Lande; Cunningham of Kirkshaw; Fergusson of Craigdarroch; Hunter of Balagan; Kirk of Glenesslane, and the

Gudeman of Friar Kerse; Jardine of Apilgirth; Murray of Cockpool, and of Morayquhat; Carruthers of Holmendes, and of Wormanbie; the Laird of Knock; and the Gudeman of Granton and of Boidisbek. There were also twenty "chief men of name, not being lairds," Adam Carlile of Bridekirk, Alexander Carlile of Eglisfechan, Edward Irving of Bonshaw, Lang Ritchie's Edward, John, the young Duke, Chrystie's Dick, Chrystie the Cowquhat, Willie of Gretna Hill (all these were Irvings), Roger Rome, Mickle Sandie Rome, David Gass, John Gass, Michil's son in Rig, George Grahame, Arthur Grahame, Richie Grahame, Will Bell, John Bell, Andro Bell, Matthie Bell, Will Bell of Redkirk, Young Archie Thomson, and Sym Thomson. A gudeman was a tenant who did not own the estate on which he lived.

"The Sheriffdoms, Stewardships, and Bailiwicks of Scotland," wrote Speed, in the reign of James VI., "are for the most part inheritary unto honourable families." Early in the year 1600 there was a constant interchange of letters respecting the incursions of the Grahames and Armstrongs on both the Scottish and English territories, and Johnstone had interviews with Lord Scrope and his deputy, Mr Lowther, to concert measures for their arrest. On the 7th of April, 1601, Nicolson informs Cecil of the redress he had demanded of the King of Scots for Border disorders, and encloses this letter from James VI., to Johnstone, dated Holyrood House, March 31, 1601:--

"Right trusty friend, we greet you heartily well. Albeit by sundry our former letters, we earnestly willed you to keep good rule and quietness in the country, and specially to stay all attempts by the broken men and thieves within your bounds upon England to the disturbing of the peace now in the dangerous time; yet perceiving you not to be so careful therein as your duty and charge required, in respect of the continual complaints still made to us of the daily incursions of the broken men committing burnings, thefts, taking of prisoners, and such like attempts in England, we cannot but impute the blame to you, who neither stayed the same nor gave us any advertisement of your inability so to do, that we ourselves might have taken care and order therein. We cannot be content that those people our neighbours shall be overcome with such rated thieves and rebellious sinners, and that the peace shall be endangered, and therefore we have given liberty to your opposites (the English Wardens) of the Middle and West March to take the opportunity of the outlaws, and rebel murderers of our late Warden, and of all such other notorious sinners, disturbers of the peace and countries, of such incursions within England, for whom you will not answer and give justice, and to pursue, take, or stir them at their advantage either in England or Scotland, without having any answerable or honest subject unless in their own default of being in company, assisting or defending the rebels, who in that case we will not hold our subjects which we have thought good to signify to you, and according to our former directions to desire you to concur with your opposites in that case, and in all other things that may stay and repress the unhappy and wicked course of these rebellious outlaws about which we look yet for a better proof of your care and good will, pursue them with fire and sword, and forbid them rest or comfort within our realm under pain of death, for we have promised to your opposites to cause the same be done by you with all diligence, and so resting persuaded to find your amendment in anything ye have overseen or lacked hitherto in your matters touching us so nearly as ye tender our favour and good will, and other ways will be acceptable to us upon your duty and obedience, we commit you to God. "JAMES R.."

Nicolson also wrote to the Laird of Johnstone, and received this answer from him:—"After my commendations in lawful manner, I received your letter wherein I perceive ye think I do not my duty in meeting your officers for the taking of good order anent the punishment of six malefactors as trouble both the countries. I assure you it has been the thing I have been most careful of ever since I accepted this office, and to that effect have craved oft and divers times meetings of my Lord Scrope, and could never get none as yet, but ever deferring answers which I sent to his Highness, the King's Majesty, both my request and his answers, which I doubt not you have seen. His Highness nor ye neither can put no fault to me, for I assure ye, the Lord Scrope is the wite of all done since my acceptance of office, and about meeting them that he left behind him in his room, I can have no certainty, because they are changed every fifteen days, and if ever I get a meeting set down with them that wrote to me last those are changed and others put in their room; wherefore I must earnestly desire you to cause a special man to be appointed that will remain still, and that the Border fears, for they will do nothing, for none of them that has been in my lord's room. I have taken some special Border men of the clan of Armstrong, and have them in sure custody, and that for the performance of such attempts as they have committed against England, and have likewise charged the whole Borders to be before me on Saturday to come, where I shall take such like order as His Majesty has given direction, providing that I may receive the like; so I commit you to God.

"Of the Loughwood, 9th April, 1601, your friend in lawful manner, "JOHNSTONE."

Nicolson enclosed this letter to Sir Robert Cecil, asking him to "take care of the West Border, for if your Honour do not it will breed worse. The Laird writes for a resident and a man that will be feared, Johnstone hath done great service in taking these men, and he would be thanked. He hath sent the word of it and prays him to send warrant to keep them, and not to deliver them unless for justice to England, notwithstanding any warrants to be after written in the contrary; a square and honest meaning in the Laird. I beseech your honour consider well of those Borders; my Lord Scrope thinks much for my plain writing, and will think more if he knows I send this. Would God he had been as his father was, then I had had his favour the more if I had made him such service."

On April 11th, Nicolson writes that "Francis Armstrong and others, the late spoilers, have been taken by the Laird of Johnstone, and recommends that they may be delivered up to Her Majesty's officers." On the 22d he encloses a letter from James VI., "by which your honour may see how he storms at me for importunities, or rather diligence to the full of my mean wit, to commend the amendment of those things to his good consideration. Anent his writing that at my desire, he sent David Murray to the Laird of Johnstone to see and advertise if there was any need of his presence. Indeed, I would the King earnestly go in person, and so did Johnstone, by letters which seeing it would not be I dealt with him to send some of his own to charge Johnstone to do diligence, so that the thieves might see that their misrule displeased him, and should be punished. But now the Border is quiet through Johnstone's diligence, who hath gotten the best of the rest of the thieves, had met Mr Lowther, meets him again for justice, and keepeth those thieves to do justice with, as the King shall be pleased, which he will obey. So as there is no fault in Johnstone; no doubt but these late disorders shall redress and all be quiet."

Chapter Nine

On April 26, 1601, James VI. wrote to inform Lord Mar of his conference with the Laird of Johnstone and Robert Scot "respecting incursions by the English on the Borders, and in regard to the delay which had taken place in staying the same through the absence of Lord Scrope from his Wardenry; that a complaint was to be sent to the Queen, our dearest sister," pointing out the sloth of Lord Scrope, and asking that a fresh man should be appointed, such as his father was; that "the murderers of the Laird of Carmichael had been protected by the English, for some of them being pursued by our Counsellor, the commendator of Holyrood House, and the Laird Johnstone, were not only openly received in full daylight by the Grahames of Esk (Englishmen), but fortified and assisted in such sort by them as they fled in fear, that they came back in company with the said outlaws and turned a chase upon our Counsellor and Warden, pursuing them so that they narrowly escaped with their lives. We are certified by our Warden that the said fugitives and outlawed Armstrongs have their residence now for the most part in Geordie Sandie's house, an Englishman." Two days later, Nicolson wrote to Cecil that the King "has had secret speeches with Johnstone," and in August reports another raid on the Borders, and that he cannot see how the peace will be preserved there. He writes soon after that Ninian Armstrong's house has been thrown down by the King's orders, and George Sandie Grahame been delivered up by the English to the Scots; and on May 25, 1602, that the outlawed Armstrongs—Carmichael's murderers—"have the last week ridden upon the Laird of Johnstone's lands, and carried away some of his goods, and the other Armstrongs would not rise to follow the rest, which the Laird takes evil, and intends to take amends as he may. This I hear, and I do fear they will in the end get life." He adds that "Johnstone and Mr Musgrave, Lord Scrope's deputy, are the only bridles that these evil men and others there have. If they miscarry, both Princes will be troubled to keep those parts in order." On November 28, 1602, he writes again—"We have here much ado about our West Border affairs, the Laird of Johnstone making odious complaints of my Lord Scrope and John of Johnstone. I see no good but evil appearance therein, yet if Lord Scrope please to take the opportunity he may have with honour, his Lordship may do anything and make the Laird seek him."[An order decreed at this time that all the constables and landed men should keep bloodhounds on the Borders to track out thieves.]

On October 25, 1602, the Laird of Johnstone, John Johnstone of Newbie, and John Johnstone of Graitney, among others, signed a bond of peace headed by the King's name. The John of Johnstone above mentioned was the son of George Johnstone, the son of William of Graitney, and Baron of Newbie.

When James VI. became King of England; in 1603, it was of the first importance that the clans on the frontier should be quelled, lest their incursions upon his new kingdom should make him unpopular with the English. He appointed Johnstone of Graitney and two colleagues to survey the debateable land and surrounding parts, with the view of placing them under large and responsible landholders; and in the State accounts for that year is a sum of £66 3s. 4d for Johnstone's expenses. A warrant, dated Westminster, January 27, 1608, also directs the Treasurer "to pay to John Johnstone of Gretna, Scotland, £100 as a free gift and reward." The Grahames were obliged to emigrate to Ireland, and a special Commission was convened, which sat for nearly eighteen years, from 1604 till 1621, to try Border causes. In 1605 James VI. wrote to the Governor of York, telling him to furnish the Laird of Johnstone with fifty more horsemen to aid in pacifying the Borders. If he had not got the money for them he was "to beg or borrow it." The result of the special Commission seems to have been that the King's favourites obtained places on it, and the greater part of the confiscated estates. In some instances they also gratified private malice. Many outlaws who well deserved it were summarily hung, but others whose crimes had been equally flagrant were spared, and even rewarded, because they had friends among the Commissioners. One of these was Robert Gordon, the heir of Lochinvar, who in 1602, in revenge for the death of a relative killed in a skirmish, made a foray through Annandale, Wamphray, Lockerbie, Reidhall, Langrigs, &c.; and killed Richard Irving of Graitney in his own house. A party of soldiers was sent to arrest him, but he took them all prisoners, and compelled the officer who commanded them to eat the King's warrant for apprehending him. He was outlawed, and a description of his personal appearance, as well as that of Lord Crichton of Sanquhar, outlawed at the same time, was sent to Carlisle and Dumfries for their apprehension. Yet only three years afterwards Gordon was made a gentleman of the King's Bedchamber, and received a gift of some confiscated estates, and in 1621 he was created a baronet. Wm. Maxwell of Kirkhouse was a similar character. In 1602 he attacked Wilkin Johnstone of Elsiechellis and John Johnstone of Husliebray, and burned their houses; and burned James Johnstone of Briggis alive in his residence. Yet in 1607 the King presented him with the Kirk lands of Kirkpatrick-Fleming, and ten years later obliged two Johnstones to sell to this Maxwell their father's land in Kirkpatrick-Fleming and Castlemilk. His brother was created Earl of Dirleton.

Douglas of Drumlanrig was made Earl of Queensberry, and Douglas of Angus was restored to his ancient honours. He was created a Marquis in 1633, and recovered some of the family estates forfeited as early as the fifteenth century.

Even the most peaceable of the smaller landed proprietors were obliged to sell, particularly if they were minors, that their estates might swell the heritage of a richer man. But though great complaints have been made of these arbitrary proceedings, it is allowed that they were effectual, and as the old poet, Scot of Satchells, sang—

On that Border was the Armstrongs able men,
Somewhat unruly, and very ill to tame.

* * *

But since King James the Sixth to England went;
There has been no cause of grief;
And he that hath transgressed since then,
Is no freebooter, but a thief.

* * *

Adieu! my brother Annan thieves,
That helpit me in my mischievs.
Adieu! Grossars, Nickson, and Bells;
Oft have we fair owrthreuch the fells.
Adieu! Robsons, Howis, and Pylis,
That in our craft has mony wilis;
Littlis, Trumbells, and Armstrongs.
Adieu! all thieves that we belongs,
Bailies, Irwynes, and Elwoods (Elliots),
Speedy of flight and slight of hands;
The Scots of Eskdale and the Grames,
I have no time to tell your names.

In 1612 bonds were drawn up and signed by the different clans protesting their loyalty, lamenting over the blood shed in times past, and the loss of life they had sustained from thieves and murderers within the Highlands and Borders; and promising for the future to pledge themselves for the good conduct of the Borders, as they would at once arrest and execute any such offenders. A deed preserved at Abbotsford is signed by James H. Lenox, Huntlie, Montrose, Cancellarius, Angus, Herries, Caithness, Traquair, Lochnivar, Johnstone, Drumlanrig, David Scot of Stobneil. At Jedburgh, 29th March, 1612. Walter Scot of Goldielands, Walter Scot of Tuschelaw, and others are signed for, being unable to write.

The Laird of Buccleuch, who was ennobled in 1606, collected a large number of those mosstroopers and cattle drivers in the middle Marches, who, to quote Camden, knew no measure of law, but the length of their swords, and sent them to Holland for the military service of the Prince of Orange, who paid him for it; and in Berwickshire there was a demand for agricultural labour, but Annandale permanently lost much of its population, who were now bereft of their employment. The long sea coast and good anchorage between the Esk and Dumfries produced hardy fishermen at Annan, Redkirk, Locharwood, Newbie, and Saltcoats; and these were turned to account by some of the landowners in a brisk trade which grew up during the 17th century be-

Friar's Carse

tween the West of Scotland and the Isle of Man, Holland, and the West Indies. A Government vessel was kept at Dumfries, but appears to have been far from vigilant; so when high duties were put upon foreign and colonial goods, this trade degenerated into smuggling, which was extended across the Esk into England, and continued a source of great profit till comparatively recent times.

In 1600 a decree of the Lords in Council charged these chiefs with the care of the Borders:—Lord Howe, Sir James Johnstone of Dunskellie, James Johnstone of Westraw (his brother-in-law), John Johnstone of Newbie, Grierson of Lag, Kirkpatrick of Closeburn, Robert Gordon, apparent of Lochinvar, John Johnstone of Graitney, Hamilton, various Maxwells, and Scot of Buccleuch. But before the special Commission was dissolved in 1621, Newbie and Graitney had disappeared as separate baronies; the first being absorbed in the estates of Johnstone of that ilk, which joined them, and the last having returned to the barony of Comlongan and Cockpool, to which it seems to have originally belonged. John Johnstone, the young Laird of Newbie, was Provost of Annan in 1604, and obtained its recognition as a burgh from the Convention of Royal Burghs which assembled that year at Perth, and to which he sent John Galloway (uncle to the first Lord Dunkeld), and Robert Loch, bailies of Annan, as his representatives. He had already borrowed various sums of money from a relative, Edward Johnstone, a merchant in Edinburgh, when he was outlawed at the instance of his wife's uncle, Sir James Douglas of Drumlanrig, for a debt to him of 2500 marks, and in 1605 he died at Carlisle. He left seven daughters as his co-heiresses, but had settled his estate on the second, Barbara, who was married to Sir William Maxwell of Gribton, a nephew of Sir James Johnstone's wife. As the barony of Newbie was entailed on male heirs, it was claimed by the Laird of Newbie's male heir, his uncle Robert of Brigholme, who established himself in the Castle, while a lawsuit commenced on both sides. The matter was cut short by William Maxwell riding with a troop of horsemen and one or two Johnstones, including Robert's nephew, Robert Johnstone of Brume, to the Castle, where, as was stated on the trial, Robert "lay fast in bed deadly sick," and the intruders were admitted by Maxwell's wife, Barbara Johnstone, and her mother, Elizabeth Stewart, Lady Newbie, who were also residing there, into the lower hall, whence they ascended into the Laird's bedroom. Robert's brother, Edward Johnstone of Ryehill, attempted to defend him, but was shot through the body; a servant and relation, Arthur Johnstone, was wounded in the face, and they were all "thrust out of the Castle with their hands tied behind their backs." Robert Birrell alludes to the affair, March 19th, 1605. "The Maxwells came to the house of Newbies and tuick the house. In taiking of the house sundrie were wounded and hurt. They keipit the house till the gaird and heralds caused them to surrender."

William Maxwell, his wife, and his mother-in-law, were summoned to Edinburgh for trial on the 21st June, 1605, at the instance of Robert Johnstone, Edward Johnstone, his brother, and Arthur Johnstone, on whose part Sir Thomas Hamilton, the King's advocate, appeared, while on Maxwell's side his wife's uncle, Sir Alexander Stewart of Garlies, the Laird of Amisfield (Charteris), and Andrew Ker of Fenton were called as witnesses for the defence. The record of the trial is headed, "Besieging the Tower of Newbie, Shooting Pistolets, Taking Captive, &c.," and begins, "Forasmuch as albeit by divers Acts of Parliament our Sovereign Lord has prohibited the wearing of pistols and hagbuts, under certain pains, notwithstanding it is of truth that such is the wicked disposition of some persons which, preferring their own revenge to the due reverence and obedience of his Highness's laws, they and their domestic servants daily and continually bear and wear pistols, swords, and hagbuts as their ordinary and accustomed weapons. . . . As viz., the said William Maxwell of Gribton, Barbara Johnstone his spouse, and Elizabeth Stewart her mother, having this long time borne a secret and hidden malice against the said Robert Johnstone of Newbie, in respect of the depending of certain acts before the Lords and Sessioners of Council," &c. The trial continued a week, and was then prorogued till the third of July, when the defendants were bound, under pain of 200 marks, to come up for judgment within fifteen days. Robert Johnstone returned to Newbie, when his land was overrun by some of Maxwell's people; on which Lord Herries, at the instance of John Johnstone, advocate, summoned Maxwell to appear (October, 1605), and Sir James Johnstone of Dunskellie and Robert of Newbie at the same time prosecuted Elizabeth Stewart, Lady Newbie, and her second husband, Samuel Kirkpatrick of Hoddam, who on their non-appearance before the Court were outlawed. Lady

Newbie appealed against this decision, and Robert Johnstone died the following December, leaving two sons, William and Edward, both minors. Various suits were carried on by young William's guardian, his uncle, Edward Johnstone of Ryehill, which extended through the year 1606; when William having also died, Sir James Johnstone of Dunskellie bought from Barbara Johnstone her own and her husband's right to the Newbie barony.

The compact was signed at Dornoch, Jan. 23, 1607; and Sir James agreed to pay 25,000 marks, and to bring up Barbara's six sisters—Janet, Mary, Agnes, Christina, Elizabeth, and Jeanette—in his own house, charging himself with their education and ultimate marriage, "as befits ladies of their degree." Their mother appears once more with her husband, Kirkpatrick, in an action against James Murray of Cockpool, in 1610, for "non-payment of certain dues."

Among the list of Border proprietors in 1624, "Edward Johnstone of Newbie" is recorded, for though Newbie at that time belonged to the Laird of Johnstone, he and his relatives continued for the rest of their lives to be called either of Newbie or of the parts of the estate where they were settled as kinsmen without legal agreements, but with a "kyndlie" right; as Abraham Johnstone of Milnebie and Brume, and his sons Robert, John, William, and Thomas of Brume; Edward Johnstone of Ryehill Castle, living in Mylnefield, and his son and grandson, both John Johnstones of Mylnefield; and David Johnstone of Robgill.

In 1573 the Laird of Johnstone was fined £2000 and outlawed for not producing John Johnstone of Graitney, who had been summoned by the Privy Council to make compensation "for all attempts committed by himself, his bairns, and servants in time past;" and the laird had acted as his pledge; but, like so many penalties adjudged to Border chiefs, it was probably never enforced, as the two families seem to have continued good friends. In 1602 John Johnstone of Graitney made a complaint to the Privy Council that having sent "his three sons, with nine of his servants, with carriage and provision, to the hunting at Liddell in England, having obtained licence so to do, for some venison for the banquet made by his chief, the Laird of Johnstone, at the late baptism of his son. It is of verity that Thomas Trumble of Mynto, Hector Trumble of Barnhill, and Mack Trumble of Bewbie," attacked and robbed them; the carriage, bedding, and victuals being worth £240.

In 1612, Graitney was confirmed by Crown charter in the possession of this John Johnstone, and allusion is made in the charter to the burning, slaughter, and devastation of these parts. Nisbet in a heraldry, compiled by order of the British Government in 1722, speaks of Johnstone of Graitney as "another cadet of Johnstone of that ilk. On an old stone on the front of the house of Graitney, of the date 1598, is the shield of arms of Johnstone of that ilk, with the addition of two mullets." In 1606 this John of Graitney gained a suit which had lasted several years over the sons of the murdered Richard Irving, who had obtained the lands of Sarkbrig and Conheath, in Graitney, on mortgage from John's grandfather, William Johnston of Newbie, and were now obliged to give them up. But in 1618 he, by royal command, sold the whole Graitney estate with the consent of his son William, and of his relatives, Edward of Ryehill and David of Robgill, to Sir John Murray of Cockpool, who had married the daughter of Gilbert Johnstone, a merchant in Edinburgh.

The Kirk land of Kirkpatrick-Fleming which had belonged to Robert Johnstone of Newbie was conferred on William Maxwell of Kirkhouse by a royal charter dated Whitehall, Jan. 10, 1607; and Brigholme and Northfield, the property of the same Laird, were sold by his son Robert, in 1610, to Mr Patrick Howat, one of the King's chaplains, afterwards a Scotch Bishop.

Sir William Maxwell of Gribton died in 1621, leaving an eldest son John. His branch of the family were still Romanists, and his youngest son, Alexander, appears on the list of Scotch students at the Douay College in France in 1622; Barbara Johnstone, Lady Gribton, being at that time resident in Paris. She had been put to the horn— i.e., proclaimed an outlaw — for "holding Papistical opinions," as the Act states, in 1616; as well as two of her sisters, Agnes Johnstone, spouse of William Lawrie, and Janet, married to John Browne in Lochhill. Lady Gribton appears to have returned to Scotland in 1628, for in August of that year James Johnstone of that ilk appeared in person, and became security for Dame Barbara Johnstone, Lady Gribton, that "the said Dame Barbara, within the space of one month after this date, shall depart and pass forth of the kingdom, and that within 22 days thereafter she shall pass forth of the bounds of Great Britain, and that she shall not return again without his Majesty's licence under the pain of 5000 marks; and the said Dame Barbara appearing personally, acted herself that during her remaining within this kingdom she shall not receive Jesuit seminary priests, nor trafficking Papists, nor shall travel about the country under the pain of 5000 marks, Sir James and his heirs becoming her cautioners."

By the acquisition of Newbie and Stapleton, Sir James Johnstone connected his lands, for he had previously been obliged to pass through Newbie's property to reach some of his own estates. Two years earlier he became possessed of the barony of Corry, and in 1599 he had turned the Johnstones of Lockerbie, out of their lands in Garwald, and annexed them, although one of these relations, Cuthbert Johnstone, was ninety years old. Lord Maxwell, the son of his rival, who had fallen at Dryfe Sands, frequently threatened him, but as Lady Johnstone was in favour with the Court, the King intervened, and ordered Maxwell to retire to Clydesdale; and when he returned without permission in 1601, avowedly to revenge himself on Johnstone, he was imprisoned in Edinburgh Castle. Thence he escaped, but was shortly afterwards induced to sign a bond "for himself and taking burden for all others concerned," by which "he forgave and remitted all hatred, rancour, &c., against Sir James Johnstone for the slaughter of John Lord Maxwell, his father, and all other slaughters and insolences which followed thereon." As he continued in disgrace, his cousin, Sir Robert Maxwell of Orchardstone, Johnstone's brother-in-law, arranged a meeting between the two chiefs—though it was to be as secret as possible— in which Maxwell was to ask for Johnstone's intercession with the King, and all old grudges were to be wiped away. Sir James took his servant, a relation,

William Johnstone, and Maxwell brought Charles Maxwell of Kirkhouse—a circumstance which made Johnstone place reliance on his good faith, as he was a nephew of John Murray of Cockpool, whose brother Charles was married to a Johnstone of Newbie. They met on horseback in a secluded spot near Tinwald (April 6, 1608), and while the two Lairds were conversing with apparent amity, Charles Maxwell entered into a warm discussion with William Johnstone and suddenly fired his pistol at him. William tried to return it, but his pistol missed fire. He shouted treason, and Sir James turning round was shot in the back by Maxwell, who at once rode away, and said he had done enough, when his second advised him not to leave William Johnstone alive. Sir James was propped up on his horse, but had only strength to say "Lord have mercy on me—Christ have mercy on me—I am deceived," before he expired. Maxwell fled to the Continent, and the case was tried in Edinburgh, June 24, 1609, by a special Parliament, which found him guilty of high treason for slaying the Warden of the Marches, and all his goods were to be confiscated. He remained abroad till 1612, when he ventured to land in Caithness, but he was treacherously seized and delivered up by his cousin's husband, Lord Caithness, and sent a prisoner to Edinburgh Castle.

By the King's order, the Laird of Johnstone, his guardian (Robert Johnstone of Raecleuch, his second cousin), his mother, and his grandmother, "the auld Lady Johnstone, were asked if they persisted in the pursuit of their petition, craving justice to be executed upon the forfeited Lord Maxwell for the slaughter of the late Lord of Johnstone;" and they said that they did. Lord Maxwell's brother presented this appeal to their mercy—"Offers of submission made by me, sumtyme Lord Maxwell, for myself, and in name of my kin and friends to. . . now Laird Johnstone, and his tutors and curators, Dame Sara Maxwell, Lady Johnstone younger for the time, his mother; Dame Margaret Scot, Lady Johnstone elder, his gudedame, and to their kin and friends, for the unhappy slaughter of the late Sir James Johnstone of that Ilk, knight, by me." After asking forgiveness of the Almighty and of the King, he proceeded to offer his bond and sworn faith that he will forgive the slaughter of his own father by the late Laird of Johnstone and his accomplices, and that it shall never be brought up against any of them again. He then proposes "to marry . . . Johnstone, daughter of the late Sir James, as owing to the sudden and unhappy slaughter of her father, she is left unprovided with a sufficient dower," and that he would require none (Lady Maxwell had died during his exile); and for the better avoiding of all future enmity between the houses of Maxwell and Johnstone "he desires the Laird of Johnstone may be married to Dame Maxwell, eldest daughter to Lord Herries, and sister's daughter to me, a person of like age with the Laird of Johnstone," and he would pay her twenty thousand Scotch merks as dower; and that, "for the further satisfaction of the house of Johnstone," he would consent to be exiled for another seven years, and longer if it was the Laird's pleasure.

Maxwell seems not only to have been ignorant of the Christian name of the young lady whom he offered to marry, and of her brother the Laird, but also of that of his own niece, from the blanks left in the MS. His petition was disregarded, and he was condemned to lose his head at the Market Cross of Edinburgh on May 20th, 1613. He refused to avail himself of the services of a minister, being a Roman Catholic, but met his death heroically. Four years later his attainder was reversed, and as he only left a daughter Janet, married to John Corsane (Provost of Dumfries in 1621), his title went to his brother Robert, who, in 1620, was created Earl of Nithsdale.

John Corsane was reputed, to be the richest commoner in Scotland. He was the twelfth generation of a family long settled at Dumfries, and of which the chiefs for eighteen generations in succession all bore the name of John. The male line became extinct in 1777.

The Johnstones of Westraw begin to reappear in Dumfriesshire affairs early in the 17th century. The Laird of Westraw married a sister of Sir James Johnstone of Dunskellie, by which he probably obtained some land in the county, as in 1600 he is among those charged with the care of the Borders. In 1608 his name was joined with that of his nephew, the young Laird of Johnstone, Agnes and Elizabeth, daughters, and Robert of Raecleuch, executor of the late Sir James, in the petition for vengeance on Lord Maxwell, and in 1617 with that of Edward Johnstone of Ryehill and several Murrays as curator to the young Laird. In 1624 Westraw sold his estates in Lanarkshire to Sir James Carmichael, afterwards Lord Hyndford, and purchased the lands of Glendinning in Dumfriesshire, to which he gave the name of Westerhall from his former estate. His great-grandson, John Johnstone, was made a baronet of Nova Scotia, April 25, 1700, with a destination to his heirs male; so as he left only one daughter, Philadelphia, the title descended to his brother William, the ancestor of the present Sir Frederick Johnstone, of the Johnstones of Alva, [John, fourth son of Sir J. Johnstone, third Bart. of Weaterhall born 1734) entered H.E.I.C.S. and commanded the Artillery at the Battle of Plassey. He bought Alva and Hangingshawe. His son James Raymond Johnstone (died 1830), left eight sons and seven daughters. James, his heir (died 1887). John, his second son, went down with half his regiment between Madras and Rangoon. John A. Johnstone now of Alva (born 1847).] and of Lord Derwent.

The son of the murdered Laird of Johnstone was raised to the peerage in 1628, by the title of Lord Johnstone of Lochwood, and was created Earl of Hartfell in 1643 by Charles I. He adhered to the Royal cause during the Civil War, and was imprisoned and his estates sequestered; but on the accession of Charles II., his son James was restored to his lands and honours; and on the death of Murray, Earl of Annandale, without direct heirs, exchanged his title of Hartfell for that of Annandale, and obtained a grant of the hereditary Stewardship of Annandale and the office of hereditary Constable of the Castle of Lochmaben. In 1701 William Johnstone, second Earl of Annandale and third of Hartfell, was created Marquis of Annandale by letters patent to him and to his heirs male whatsoever, a title which has been in abeyance since 1792, when his last son, George, third Marquis of Annandale, died childless. It is now claimed by Mr Hope-Johnstone, the descendant of Charles, Earl of Hopetoun, who married the sister of the last Marquis, by Colonel Sir James Johnstone, the representative of the Johnstones of Newbie Castle, and by Sir Frederick Johnstone of Westerhall.

In 1609 an Act of Parliament was passed at Edinburgh, stating that "our Sovereign Lord, King James, for the support of the Town of Annan, which is miserably impoverished so as not to be able to build a kirk to themselves, has granted and disponed to the said town and parochin the house called the Castle of Annan, the hall and tower thereof, to serve for a kirk and place of convening to the hearing of the word and ministration of the Sacraments."

The Johnstones of Wamphray died out in the male line in 1657, and their estate was ultimately bought by Dr John Rogerson, a native of the place, who at an early age went to Russia as chief physician to the Empress Catherine II., whom he attended on her deathbed. He remained attached to the Russian Court till 1816, when he returned to Dumfriesshire, and died in 1823, being buried in Wamphray churchyard. He had been preceded in his post by two Dumfriesshire men, Dr Halliday and Dr Mounsay; and a member of the Crichton family, Sir Alexander Crichton, succeeded him as physician to the Emperor Alexander I., and went through the Russo-French campaign of 1812-13-14.

On the marriage of the late Emperor Nicolas with a Princess of Prussia in 1817 he was appointed physician to the future Empress, but a member of her own family at last interfered when she had been in bad health for many months, on the ground that he was old-fashioned in his practice and too fond of the lancet. He therefore resigned his Court appointment, but continued for some time at St. Petersburg. He died in Kent in 1856.

In 1610 the Justices of the Peace for Dumfriesshire and the Stewartry of Annandale were John, Earl of Wigtown (who married the widow of Sir J. Johnstone, killed by Maxwell), Robert Lord Crichton, Alexander, Laird of Garlies, William Lord Cranstoun, Sir James Douglas of Drumlanrig, Sir John Charteris of Amisfield, Grier of Lag, Robert Douglas of Cassogill, Sir Thomas Kirkpatrick of Closeburn, Wemyss of Cassogill, Murray of Cockpool, Robert Johnstone of Raecleuch, tutor of Johnstone, Carruthers of Holmains, Mr John Johnstone, John Johnstone of Graitney, Sir Robert Dalzell of Knock, and Edward Johnstone of Ryehill Castle.

The eldest son of Sir William Maxwell of Gribton appears in 1628 as taking out letters of slain against Johnstone of Willis, who had murdered William Johnstone (he was natural son to the last John Johnstone, baron of Newbie) in the town of Johnstone, near Lochwood. John Maxwell, the pursuer, is called his sister's son, and nearest of kin to the deceased. The case shows what an imperative duty this action was on behalf of a murdered man, and also that this kind of connection was legally recognised as a relation in Scotland, though it never was in England.

Chapter Ten

During twenty-four years after the purchase of the Barony of Newbie by Sir James Johnstone, there were legal actions regularly twice every year to expel the relatives of the last owner and their dependants, and to enforce the payment of their taxes and tithes. At that time in Scotland farms were usually held by one man in feu, and portions of them were sublet to five or six tenants, who were all held responsible for the rent. Sir James had died much in debt, partly owing to having acted as cautioner for relatives, and his creditors laid claim to Newbie, and obtained decreets to compel Robert Johnstone of Raecleuch, who took up his abode at Newbie Castle as guardian of the young laird; Edward Johnstone of Ryehill; his brothers David and Abraham; his sons Adam and John Johnstone of Mylnfield; his grandson John, the younger, and many nephews to quit the estate, besides the Irvings, Gibson the ploughman, and others, who seem to have been small tenants, and whose names are still found in these parts, Farcis Pott, Wilkin, &c. The names vary in these summonses as time went on, and some died, and others grew up. John Johnstone of Mylnfield was Sheriff-Depute of Dumfries, and infefted the young Laird of Johnstone in part of his property in 1609. In 1611 his name is omitted, and a seasine describes Galabank, where he was living the previous year, as bounded on one side by "an estate of the late Robert Johnstone, called of Newbie, which John Johnstone, [He is called John Johnstone, son and heir apparent of the late --- Johnstone of Newbie, in "Thomas Corrie of Kelwood and Newbie against the occupiers of Newbie." 1630.] the son of the late John Johnstone in Mylnfield, now occupies." Then the proceedings are carried on against his widow Bessie and her son George, and against his eldest son, John Johnstone, even after the last moved into Annan, where we find him owning a "vast stone house" on the site of the old Tolbooth, once Bruce's Castle, and which had lately been occupied by Edward Johnstone of Ryehill, who was married in 1614 to Barbara Udward of Castlemilk. She was the rich widow of Mr John Johnstone, late Commendator of Holywood, and they removed to Edinburgh and Castlemilk, where she owned houses. She died in 1621, and the next year Edward Johnstone was again living in the vast stone house at Annan, and John, his grandson, in another belonging to Gaylies Rig, whom he had lately married, but still owning land in Mylnfield. In 1630 John is termed "callit of Newbie" (though on other occasions he is called "of Mylnfield" to the rest of his life), when he was summoned in company with Barbara Johnstone, Lady Gribton, Edward Johnstone of Seafield (son to the late Robert of Newbie), Thomas Corry of Kelwood, Edward Johnstone of Ryehill, James Johnstone of Westerhall, James, his son, Viscount Drumlanrig, and David Johnstone of Edinburgh, by the Earl of Nithsdale as Sheriff to show their title-deeds to the Newbie estate. Murray of Dundrennan, Sir Robert Douglas of Torthorwald, and the Commissioners for settling the Borders all in turn summoned them, and of course the relatives of Newbie, the kyndlie tenants, had none to show.

This is the last time that the name of Edward Johnstone of Seafield, the heir of the Newbies, appears, and he probably died soon afterwards. Nine years before he had been assaulted in the streets of Dumfries, and left for dead, but had been picked up by Patrick Young, surgeon, passing that way, and revived. He had carried many suits before the courts of law against his uncle and guardian and the Laird of Johnstone to put him in possession of the property of his ancestors, but never appears to have married.

Edward Johnstone of Ryehill had been guardian to his nephew during his minority, and also one of the curators or guardians of the young Laird of Johnstone; and in 1619 the Laird, and the Earls of Mar, Lothian, and Buccleuch, Lord Crichton, Sir John Murray, and James Johnstone of Lochens, also his curators, brought an action against him and against Robert Johnstone of Raecleuch and James Johnstone of Westerhall to recover the Annandale charter chest, which was in Edward Johnstone's charge. It was restored by Lady Wigton, the Laird's mother, to whom Edward had transferred it, though it contained important papers connected with the Newbie family which have never been recovered by the heirs of the original owners. The year before, Edward Johnstone had joined with the other curators in an action to compel Robert to turn out of Newbie and give it up to the young Laird, and also to render some account of the estate. In 1621 Edward Johnstone of Ryehill ejected Robert, his wife, and children from the Castle, [In 1650 Fergus Grahame of Blaatwood, son-in-law of Robert Johnstone of Raecleuch, and Sara Johnstone, his wife, bring an action against the Earl of Annandale to compel him to provide sustenance for them and "their eleven poor children."] and put the young Laird in possession of it. Robert made an attempt to turn the young Laird out of Newbie, assisted by young George Johnstone of Mylnfield, and a trial ensued, but no sentence seems to have been passed; and Robert, the principal defendant, was cautioner for the rest. An action was brought in 1617 against young John Johnstone of Mylnfield, and his brothers George, Edward, and David, with Thomas Carruthers, son of the Laird of Wormanbie, for carrying arms and assaulting George Weild, a tenant in Mylnfield, "while doing his lawful affairs in sober and quiet manner, looking for no violence or injury to be done unto him from any person." John Johnstone, "on his own confession," was fined ten pounds for the whole party by the Lochmaben Court, but the pursuer not being satisfied brought the case before the Lords in Council at Edinburgh, where John appeared in person and was fined forty pounds. This is one of the first causes connected with the Johnstones of Newbie or Lochwood which did not end with "oft times called, but never appeared." Another cause in 1618, which dragged on several years, was at the instance of the Provost, Bailies, and Council of Annan, who, "for the safe transport of his Majesty's subjects, and in respect of the great poverty of the said burgh, had kept a boat and exacted dues, and now John Johnstone, burgess of Annan, also called John of Mylnfield, and others, would not let it pass their land." This action was brought in 1628 before the Lords in Council, and the offenders not appearing, were outlawed, a sentence declared to be "wrongful," by the Justiciary Court at Dumfries, and not acted on. The parson and minister of Moffat, Mr Walter Whitford, at the same time brought an action against the young Laird of Johnstone for unlawfully convoking his kin and friends, among whom were two of the Newbie family, and assaulting people in Moffat. The relatives of the Border chiefs being no longer employed in war were constantly being cited for offences of this description, and they seem to have had a perfect passion for litigation.

In the cases of sequestration or compulsory sale on the Borders under the auspices of the Royal Commission there seems to have been some pretext of a charter granted a hundred years before to the incoming possessor, or some marriage into the family of the old owners; but this occasionally resulted in three or four claimants being infefted in the same estate. Mr Patrick Howat, one of the King's chaplains, was infefted by Royal Charter in the lands of Galabank, Hardriggs, Brigholme, Northfield, and Gullielands, bordering on Newbie, in 1610; but when Sir John Murray of Dundrennan called upon all in that neighbourhood to show their title deeds, John Galloway produced a resignation from Jeffrey Irving of Bonshaw (the son of Christopher, whose wife was the daughter of Johnstone of that Ilk, and was living there in 1582), infefting him in Galabank. The son of the late Robert Johnstone of Newbie produced a Royal Charter granting Brigholme, Hardriggs, &c., to his father in 1582. John Murray of Aiket showed a grant of the lands of Northfield and Gullielands under the great seal in 1604, and Ewart produced an old charter of these lands made out to a John Ewart and his wife Janet Johnstone in 1549. Thereupon Howat disposed of Galabank to Galloway (who appears to have been nephew or grandson to Christopher Irving and Margaret Johnstone) because, as he states, he had "called to mind that it is most godly and equitable that the present lands should be sold and disposed by me to the old kyndlie and native tenants and possessors of the said lands; and understanding that John Galloway, bailie burgess of Annan, and his predecessors since many ages past have been old kyndlies and native tenants and possessors of the said lands of Galabank," he herewith restores them to Galloway for an equivalent. Galloway's brother Patrick was another of the Royal chaplains, and the father of the first Lord Dunkeld. His wife was Helen Gask of Ruthwell, and their daughter, Helen Galloway, was married to William Rig, the son of Cuthbert Rig, whose signature is appended to some Maxwell, Carruthers, and Burgh of Dumfries deeds at an earlier date, and one of whose daughters or granddaughters married a Maxwell of Kirkconnell. William Rig and Helen Galloway had two daughters, the eldest married to John Irving, "called the Laird," and the younger, Gaylies or Egidia, was married first to Robert Loch, and afterwards, in 1622, to Johnstone, "called of Mylnfield," who bought Galabank or Gallowbank from his wife's grandfather in 1624.

Edward Johnstone of Ryehill is last heard of July 1, 1640, when he witnessed a bond for the Laird of Johnstone and Sir John Charteris of Amisfield at Annan. The other witnesses were Grierson of Lag and Macbriar of Dumfries.

The many lawsuits he had taken part in on behalf of his two nephews, of the young Laird, and of his stepsons, as well as on his own, impoverished him, else, from the lands he had possessed and the many times he had acted as cautioner, he must at one time have been a rich man. One field after another of his property was sold, and in 1634 he disposed of his lands in Ryehill and Cummertrees to Murray, Earl of Annandale, with the consent of Lady Wigton, the Laird of Johnstone's mother, and of her second husband. The large stone house in Annan and property in Stank seem to have been all that he had left, and these went to John Johnstone of Mylnfield, who, like Edward of Ryehill, was frequently Provost of Annan, and a member of Parliament for Dumfries.

In 1640 the friend and executor of George Heriot, the Royal jeweller, died in Edinburgh. He was the author of a large folio

Closeburn

in Latin, published at Amsterdam, on "the affairs of Britain and certain other European nations," often quoted by Sir Walter Scott. He left legacies to some of his nearer relations and the Laird of Johnstone his executor, besides bequests to Dumfriesshire charities, and a sum of money to build a bridge over the Annan. He was commemorated at Edinburgh on a tablet in the chapel of Trinity College Hospital (pulled down in 1848 to accommodate the railway) with the following inscription:— "Dr Robert Johnstone, of the house of Newbie in Annandale, an eminent lawier, among several other considerable sums left by him in anno 1640, to be improven into certain pious and charitable uses in this city, did bequeathe 18,000 merks, which, according to the laudable intention of this munificent benefactor, the good town applied for advancing the charitable and religious ends of this Hospital. By which donary, as by the many other acts of his liberality, this great donator hath propagated a lasting monument of his piety to posterity."

As Newbie Castle had suffered much in various sieges, it is believed that the Laird appropriated Robert Johnstone's legacies to add a modern structure to the old square tower. Among the Wodrow MSS. is an account of the drunken frolics of Sir John Dalziel of Glennie and his associates, which ended by going "to the Lord Annandale's house at Newbie to pay him a visit, beginning with their old pranks, burning their shirts and other linens. A little after that the house was all burnt, and it was reported of my lord himself he knew the house would never do good, for it was builded with the thing that should have builded the bridge over Annan water. It is said that the servants in the house were amusing themselves with drinking burnt brandy while Lord Annandale was away, and his coach driving suddenly to the door, they thrust the blazing spirits under a bed which caused the conflagration. The blaze was so great that the chambermaids in Sir John Douglas's house at Kelhead, three miles distant, could prepare the bedrooms without candles."

This Robert Johnstone left 18,000 marks to the College of Edinburgh, where he had been educated. He had lived in London, at Blackfriars, for many years, and added six scholarships to Heriot's Hospital to be held by Dumfriesshire boys of the name of Johnstone.

Robert Johnstone of Raecleuch was dead in August, 1627, and his son, Robert of Stapleton, died before August, 1656. The last left only a daughter married to William Irving of Stank. John Johnstone of Croghan, a physician, is reputed to have been a relative of the Annandale family. His works were published in Latin at London and Amsterdam about 1630. He dedicated a history of quadrupeds to our foreign physicians, and "Thaumatographia Naturalis," written when he was 70, to the Princes Radziwil, Count Boguslaf, and Viadislaf Monwid, all Polish nobles. Arthur Johnstone, a poet who wrote in Latin at the same period, was physician to James VI., and though born in Aberdeen, claimed kinship with Annandale. One of his poems is addressed to James Johnstone, the Laird, and another to Baron Robert. [Chalmers describes the ancient salt works which belonged to the monks on the Solway, and to the Johnstones of Newbie at Priestwode, and at Carlaverock. The first called Lady Saltcotes was then owned by the Murrays of Cockpool. In 1661 an Act of Parliament was passed in favour "of some poor people and tenants in Annan who by their industry and toilsome labour do from sand draw salt for the use of some private families in that bounds, and who in regard of the painfulness and singularity of the work have ever been free of any public imposition until the year 1656, or thereby, that the late usurper (Cromwell), contrary to all reason, equity, or former practice, forced from them an exaction to their overthrow and ruin, and thereby so impoverished them that they are in a starving condition. Therefore the Act declares the said salters wining and making salt within the bounds above specified in the manner above written to be free of any payment of excise in time coming."]

George, the eldest son of John Johnstone of Mylnfield and Galabank, married in 1643 Agnes Grahame, a descendant of the Laird of Johnstone, who died in 1567. George died in 1649, leaving two sons John and Edward. Their mother was re-married to Robert Fergusson of Hallhill, and had a daughter Agnes, afterwards the wife of Mr Orr. John Johnstone of Mylnfield was dead in 1665, and his grandson John inherited Galabank, near Annan, "the vast stone house" in Annan, Closehead, and the lands of Stank.

Two years earlier he had mortgaged them in anticipation to his uncle, Robert Grahame of Inglistoune. He redeemed them (March 14, 1672) owing to his marriage with Janet Kirkpatrick, of Auldgirth (at Dumfries, Feb. 2, 1670), having brought him an accession of fortune. The marriage contract is signed by Galabank's mother, his grandfather Grahame, and the bride's cousin, Sir Thomas Kirkpatrick. The bridegroom settled his property on his wife and their children, and she made over to him 300 marks given to her by Sir Thomas, and everything else in her possession. Galabank was made a bailie of Annan, but was not much there, to judge from his letters and deeds, which are dated from Ruthwell, Lochmaben, and a variety of places. In 1673 he again raised a loan from Bryce Blair, the ex-Provost of Annan, and in 1677 from his brother Edward. In 1682 letters of inhibition were raised against him at the instance of Bryce Blair to prevent him from disposing of any property till he had paid his debts. The next year he mortgaged Galabank and Stank to his brother, who was on his part to satisfy the creditors, particularly William Grahame of Blaatwood, Provost of Annan (owed £373 9s sterling); and Grahame received his first instalment of interest, £22 7s, at once. But in 1684 William Craik of Arbigland was the most urgent creditor, and a warrant was issued in the King's name (James VII.) directing the Sheriffs of Annandale to denounce John Johnstone as a rebel from the market-place of Lochmaben, and to seize all his moveable goods and gear. The Sheriffs and other officials seem to have taken no notice of it, for another was addressed in 1689 in William and Mary's name to the sheriffs, bailies, and stewards of the Borders, directing them to seize upon John Johnstone "who continues and abides under the process of our said horning unslaved, and in the meantime daily and openly haunts, frequents, and repairs to kirks, markets, fairs, and other public and private places of meeting within this our realm as if he were our free liege, in high and proud contempt of this our authority and laws, and giving thereby evil example to others to do and commit the like in time coming without remedies be thereto provided as is alleged," &c. The letter of horning, as it is called, adds that he is to be put in sure ward in "a tolbooth" (prison), and detained there night and day at his own expense, and if need be kyves or handcuffs were to be used for that purpose. These letters of horning were issued twice every year without any effect. John Johnstone's wife died in 1680, leaving two daughters, Janet and Barbara. He married secondly Elizabeth Murray, a connection, being one of the Murrays of Cockpool. She survived him, and left no children. He is mentioned last in a deed of May, 1704, when he was dead. Barbara was also dead, but the marriage certificate of Janet Johnstone shews that she was married Jan., 1706, by the Rev. Edward Wilshire, according to the laws of the Church of England, at Kirkandrews-upon-Esk, in Cumberland, to Richard Beattie of Milleighs, in the same parish, where her father probably retired, as in 1698 "letters of poynding and horning" were registered against the Provost of Annan (the first Marquis of Annandale) and the bailies for permitting John Johnstone to retain possession of his house and goods, and to go about "unslaved," though he still did not leave Annan till 1701.

His brother Edward (a Writer to the Signet) married in 1683 Isobelle, daughter of Adam Carlyle, [Barbara, daughter of John Johnstone of Mylnfield and Galabank, married in 1648 Lancelot Carlile at Dumfries. His elder brother Adam seems to have been this Adam's father.] whose family has been already mentioned as descended from a sister of Robert Bruce. Carlyle was a landed proprietor, and a bailie of Annan, and endowed his daughter with a house possessing yards, meadows, mosses, moors, &c., according to the description given in the title-deed. Galabank was one of the witnesses to the marriage contract. The bride was fifteen, and her husband forty. Edward Jobnstone left Dumfries about this time, and came to live in Annan, where his eldest son John was born in 1688, and baptised May 27, 1689; also James, born in 1693, and three daughters, Janet, Marie, and Elizabeth. He was treasurer for the burgh for ten years, and his executors obtained a receipt from the magistrates in 1706 setting forth the honourable manner in which he had fulfilled his trust. He left provision for his family when he died (Dec. 30, 1697), aged fifty-four, although both his brother and the burgh of Annan were much in his debt. His will is dated three days before his death, and begins with a confession of the Christian faith. He gives his house property (burdened with an annuity to his wife, but only to continue during her widowhood) and 300 marks to his eldest son John. To his three daughters he left 400 marks each, and to his youngest son James 300 marks, the last to succeed to his house property if John died without heirs. If any of the debts due to him were recovered, the sum was to be divided between his two sons and his nephew George Johnstone, whom he left co-executor with his brother-in-law James Carlyle, and he charged both "to act as the protectors of his wife and children, to see them righted in what belongs to them as far as they can." In the event of the death of his children without heirs his lands were to go to James Carlyle. He directed that his body should be decently buried in the churchyard at Annan. His will was witnessed by Robert Colville, James Carruthers, John Irving, and George Blair.

Soon after Edward Johnstone's death, his brother paid a small portion of his debt to the widow, who in 1704 obtained from the first Marquis of Annandale a "precept of poynding" against two of the tenants on the Galabank estate, which had been made over to a relative in London, to oblige them to pay some rents overdue to her and her children, instead of paying them to their landlord. But in 1708 the Londoner died intestate, so the Government claimed Galabank, Stank, and his other estates as its due. A protest was raised by Janet Johnstone, who asserted her right to them, as they had been settled on her mother, and her mother's children, of whom she was now the sole survivor. Her cause was advocated at Edinburgh before the Lords of Council and Session, and decided in her favour, and the order of the Chancellery infefting her with the estates is dated March 1st, 1709. Anticipating this decision she had mortgaged Galabank to her cousin John Johnstone for the sum still unpaid, which had been borrowed by her father from his brother. John, the younger, exchanged money he had never received for lands his cousin never really held, and was to pay one penny a year as an acknowledgment to Janet, who might redeem the mortgage at any future time; but this plan was overturned

Jan. 4, 1711, by a decision of the Lords in Council in favour of the Londoner's creditors. She made a second appeal against this verdict, while a counter appeal was lodged on behalf of Joseph Corrie, to whom Galabank had been mortgaged by her father.

The possession of the estates was hotly contested, to judge by numerous items in the lawyer's bills; John Carlyle of Limekilns and Richardson of Edinburgh on one side, and John Hair and Richardson of Annan on the other. John Boswell of Auchinleck was also employed. In addition to the causes mentioned eleven legal processes, instituted by various claimants, seem to have ruined all concerned in them except the lawyers. John Johnstone lent his cousin Janet money to carry them on, and on Oct. 10, 1713, was married to a wife with a fair dowry, Anna Ralston, [Ralston of that Ilk is found in Lanarkshire, 1530.] the daughter of the deceased William Ralston (related to the Lockharts of Lee) and Janet Richardson of Hichill, his wife. In the marriage contract 200 marks a year, a fourth of the value of the lands of Galabank, was settled on Anna Ralston (Jan. 3, 1714). He bought off Joseph Corrie's claims to Galabank with £1000 Scots money, still owed to Corrie, but was immediately sued by Robert Carruthers, another creditor. Before this time, in return for what John had lent to her, which she had no hope of paying, Janet and her husband renounced their claim to Galabank in favour of John, who was to take upon himself all further obligations connected with the estate except a small annuity to Elizabeth Murray, Janet's stepmother, which she still engaged to pay. She declared on oath before the bailies of Annan that she ceded this estate with that of Stank to her cousin, being no ways courted or compelled to do so. Her renunciation is signed by George Blair, notary, John Irving, Joseph Irving, John Johnstone Robert Johnstone, Robert Wilson, and Bryce Tennan and the deed of gift by Richard Beattie and several more. Another deed of similar import is signed by Bernard Ross, Mr John Carruthers, William Johnstone, Joseph Murray, Janet Johnstone, &c.

John Johnstone was infefted in the lands of Stank as early as May 3, 1704, on account of half of the debt due to his father. Yet after giving up all right to her father's property, Mrs Beattie was still persecuted by his creditors. She left Scotland to escape a summons to appear before the Lords of Council in 1713, and the next year John Johnstone was living on the estate of Galabank, much annoyed by trespassers, who pulled up his trees and broke down his dykes. One Sunday he attacked two or three of these intruders, and an enemy caused him to be summoned before the Kirk-Sessions and compelled him to make an apology. In 1711 he went to London, where Richard Beattie in a letter mentions that he had been for some time, and about this period he was made a bailie of Annan. In 1719 he obtained "a letter of horning and poyndling" against William Elliot of Eckleton, which called upon the defendant to warrant and acquaint and defend the said John Johnstone personally, or in his dwelling-place, against adjudications "affecting the houses and lands now in his possession within six days, the said Elliot having accused John Johnstone of being unlawfully their possessor, whereas he had received them lawfully from the heritable owners, Richard Beattie and Janet Johnstone, for certain sums of money which the said Beattie absolutely required."

At the court of the burgh of Annan, September 29, 1714, held by John Johnstone and John Irving, the following, after taking the oaths to King George, were re-elected magistrates for the ensuing year, viz.:—James Lord Johnstone (eldest son of the Marquis), Sir William Johnstone of Westerhall, eldest bailie; John Irving and John Johnstone, second and third bailies; William Irving, treasurer; John Halliday, dean. As the town of Annan acted very independently of the Edinburgh courts, the opponents of John Johnstone and his cousin had little chance of obtaining what they called their rights against the Johnstone influence in the burgh, even when they had gained their suit before the Lords in Council. But the Lords once more reversed their decision, and gave it in favour of John Johnstone in 1718, whereupon he paid off those creditors who had obliged the Beatties to leave Scotland. Richard Beattie was dead in 1718, but the case was not finally ended till 1724, when James Johnstone was deputed by his brother and his cousin Janet to make an amicable settlement with the other creditors to avert any more legal suits. On Oct. 30, James wrote to his brother, in a letter addressed "for John Johnstone of Galabank, in Annan, Dumfries Bagge, North Britain," that he had made with some expenditure an end of the whole affair, and obtained a receipt from Mrs Orr, his cousin, but a creditor, and also an order to her lawyer to deliver up into John's hands all the family papers she had received as a pledge, and the various legal documents connected with the suit. James Johnstone wrote again on Nov. 2, and stated that he was going to Chippenham. He died four and a half years later (July 23, 1729), at the Blue Anchor Inn, in Little Britain, a part of London much frequented by Scotsmen at that time. He was thirty-six, and was buried in the St. Botolph's churchyard, Aldgate, but his name is inscribed on one of the family monuments in Annan churchyard. He owned a small piece of land in Annan, which he left to his brother, but debts amounting to £340 4s English, which his brother paid. His funeral expenses were £17 4s 6d, exclusive of the luncheon at the Blue Anchor, and the bill contains items now long disused at the quiet funeral of a private gentleman, such as fourteen men with wax lights, two men with flambeaux to light the door, hire of fourteen silver sconces and satin favors. There were sixteen mourners.

The poverty of Scotland as compared with England at that date is much dwelt upon by travellers, and is shown by the very small bribes which even the Scottish Peers most opposed to the abolition of their Parliament were willing to accept in 1700, one of them being bought over to the English side with only £11, and the most exorbitant only requiring, £30. In 1704 an Englishman passing through Dumfriesshire sums up his impression of the country with the remark that if Cain had been born a Scotsman his punishment would have been, not to wander about, but to stay at home. "From Moffat," he says, "I came through Pudeen, and to Annan or Annan house, both small villages, and at the last place I dined at a good Scotch house; and so came to Lockerby, a small town, where I lay. It had rained from before noon to night, and to comfort me more my room was overflown with water, so that the people laid heaps of turf for me to tread upon, to get from the door to the fireplace, and thence to the bed, and the floor was so worn in holes that had I trod aside a turf, I might have sunk to my knees in mud and water, and no better room was to be had in this town. Nay, worse, my room had but half a door, and that to the street; and the wall was broken down at the gable, so that the room lay open to the stable. And yet the people had French wine, though it was always spoiled for want of being well cellared."

The Scots had long been famous for their wine and for their ability to consume it. "Bacchus hath great guiding here," wrote the English ambassador from Edinburgh with regard to the court, when James VI. was entertaining his wife's brother, the Duke of Holstein, in 1598. But in 1704 the Borders were certainly poorer and less populated than 100 years earlier. The Solway had increased upon the land, and thriving villages, such as Seafield, on the coast, are now only represented by a farm or a few cottages.

A Laird's wife seldom possessed more than one silk dress in her whole life, and that descended to her daughters; a maid servant's wages were 30s a year, and a footman in a nobleman's establishment much later on was well paid with £5. The wine bills were out of all proportion to the other expenditure, although wine was cheap compared to articles of food, which were dear considering their price in other countries and the high value, of money. Before the Customs were made uniform in England and Scotland, Annan was the headquarters of an extensive smuggling trade for carrying wine, brandy, and other foreign goods into Cumberland, often on men's backs concealed in loads of hay, sacks of wool, or sheafs of wheat. The coast was covered with small ships in the service of smugglers, and in 1711 a Custom-house officer writes to his superior in Edinburgh that at Ruthwell the people are such friends to the traffic, "no one can be found to lodge a Government officer for a night."

In 1714 there was an agitation throughout Dumfriesshire in expectation of the landing of the Chevalier Prince James [As Her Majesty objects to the term "Pretender" (see "More Leaves from our Life in the Highlands"), there is no need to use it.] in Scotland, which took place the next year, when for the last time the Maxwells and Johnstones were opposed to each other, Maxwell, Lord Nithsdale, heading the Jacobites, and thereby losing his title, and the Marquis of Annandale, the Lord-Lieutenant of the County, collecting the militia together on behalf of George I. Sir Robert Gordon of Lochinvar, who had been created Lord Kenmure, raised a troop at Moffat on behalf of the Chevalier and marched to join Lord Derwentwater in Cumberland, having found it impossible to take Dumfries, protected as it was by the Marquis. He was captured at Preston, and executed the same day as Lord Derwentwater—Feb. 24, 1716. Dalziell, Earl of Carnwarth, joined the Jacobites, and obtained a reprieve, but his title was attainted and not restored till 1826.

Probably the stagnation of trade and general depression had given encouragement to the Prince's advisers, but, like the expedition under his son, it failed for want of money. In 1706 the whole coinage of Scotland only amounted to £411,117 10s 9d, and of this sum £40,000 was English, and £132,080 17s in foreign coins. The Rev. Alexander Carlyle describes a visit to his relatives in Dumfriesshire in 1733. "The face of the country was particularly desolate, not having yet reaped any benefit from the union of the Parliaments; nor was it recovered from the efforts of that century of wretched government which preceded the Revolution and commenced at the accession of James VI. The Border wars and depredations had happily ceased, but the Borderers having lost what excited their actions were in a dormant state during the whole of the 17th century unless it was during the time of the great rebellions and the struggle between Episcopacy and Presbyterianism. Sir William Douglas of Kelhead, whose grandfather was a son of the Duke of Queensberry, looked like 'a grieve or barnman' in a blue bonnet over his grey hair and a hodden grey coat, but was sensible and well bred. In the evening we visited an old gentleman, James Carlyle of Brakenquhate, who had been an officer under James II., but threw up his commission rather than take the oath. His house had but two rooms above and two below, but it was full of guns and swords, and other warlike instruments."

When Pennant visited Annandale in the last century, he found the custom of hand-fisting instead of marriage still occasionally practiced, and attributes it to the time when clergy were scarce in those parts. He noticed a railed enclosure, and heard that it was a refuge for criminals and outlaws. Yet the rising in favour of Prince Charles followed these descriptions, and could only be crushed out in Scotland with the aid of Dutch and German troops. The licence which was permitted to the victorious soldiers left the northern parts of the country a famine-stricken waste, but the militia recruited in the county were again the defence chiefly relied on to secure the loyalty of Dumfriesshire, and it consequently suffered less than other parts from the cruelty and exactions of the avengers of Gladsmuir.

Chapter Eleven

In the old graveyard at Annan, where the Castle formerly stood, now built round by houses, but with a beautiful view of the river, two large monuments record the names of eleven children of John Johnstone, the fourth Laird of Galabank. [Close to them lies "ane honest memorable man callit George Johnstown, who lived in credit and commendation, and died in Christ in the year 1648. Erected to the memory of her good husband by his wife, Agnes Grahame." Below are the family arms.] Below the youngest is inscribed, "Here also is interred the venerable father of this numerous family, John Johnstone of Galabank, Esq., the representative of the Johnstones of Mylnfield and Newby Castle and an ancient cadet of the Johnstones of Johnstone. He died Oct. 12, 1774, aged 86. 'The hoary head is a crown of glory, if it be found in the way of Righteousness.'"

The eldest son, Edward, was born in 1716, matriculated at Edinburgh in 1733, and as a probationer of divinity preached several times in the College Chapel before the Professors when he was still under twenty. After taking his degree of M.A. in 1739, he was appointed tutor to the sons of the Marchioness of Annandale and her second husband, Colonel Johnstone (the eldest of whom was the first Baronet of Hackness Hall), and gave some instruction to the sons of her first marriage, George, third Marquis of Annandale, and Lord John Johnstone, residing alternately at the Marquis's seat of Comlongan and at Appleby in Westmoreland. In 1743 he was presented by the Marquis to the living of Moffat, where he died in 1761. He published an essay on the Edinburgh Review, and a volume of sermons, including one on the death of George II. William, his next brother, took the degree of M.D. at Edinburgh. In 1741 he sailed with the third son, John, to Jamaica, and in a cruise among the West Indian Islands they were captured by the Spaniards, and endured great hardships while in their hands. William died on board ship very soon after his release, at the age of twenty-five, and John never recovered an attack of fever, which deprived him of his mental powers, though he returned to Annan and lived to the age of seventy.

The biography of James, the fourth son of Johnstone of Galabank, is to be found in histories of Worcestershire (where he practised as a physician for fifty years), among "Lives of Eminent Scotsmen," and in periodicals of the time. Born in 1730, he matriculated at Edinburgh in 1746, and went to France for the completion of his medical education. As he stayed in Worcestershire on his road to Plymouth, whence he embarked for Havre, an influential resident induced him to make that county the scene of his future career. From Havre he went to Paris, where Louis XV., though still but forty years old, had quite lost his early popularity; and the young man's observations on the new philosophy, the extraordinary licence of the press, combined with the tyranny and selfishness of the despotic government, in spite of splendid charitable institutions, founded by the piety of private individuals, or of earlier monarchs, foreshadowed the great Revolution which thirty-nine years later burst upon Europe. But the event of his youth was the invasion of Scotland ["Those engaged in war,"said Monthieu, quoted by Scott, "have much occasion for the mercy of the Deity, since in the exercise of their profession they are led to become guilty of so much violence towards their fellow-creatures." This might well be quoted by a Scotsman. The horrors that disgraced the triumph over the Jacobite rebellion recall the earlier wars with England when instances of cannibalism were known, for in 1746 we hear of Highland peasant women with their children begging for the offal of the bullocks requisitioned by the soldiery—the fathers, whether in arms or otherwise, having all been killed. It was these wars which made Scotland, once beautifully wooded, the barest country in Europe.] by Prince Charles in 1743, though it met with even less sympathy in Dumfriesshire than that of Prince James in 1715. Bryce Blair, late Provost of Annan, and John Johnstone, the actual Provost, each contributed £100 to a levy of £2000 exacted by the Prince's army from Annandale, and many of the poorer people produced their few shillings or even pence very readily, so that £1195 was collected in a short time. The Prince lodged at two houses in Dumfries; one is the Commercial Hotel, where he held a levee on his return from England, and the town was fined £4000 sterling for an attack made in the street on one of the Prince's Highland followers. But on his march southwards Charles went direct to Carlisle, which was feebly garrisoned by north country militia inclined to the house of Stuart, and made no resistance. The roads were so bad that some of the baggage waggons were left in the mud near Ecclefechan, and with the soldiers in charge of them were seized by a large party of citizens from Dumfries. The prisoners consisted of Highlanders armed with only pikes and scythe blades. For this service, and for the attitude of its Provost (Corsane), Dumfries received some confiscated estates from the Government.

When the Jacobite army was returning discomfited from Derby a band of volunteers undertook to guard the bridge at Annan over which it must cross, and also to intercept it at the Esk, but fled at the first sound of the pibroch. This is described by young James Johnstone, who was then fifteen, and in expectation of his father's horses being requisitioned he took them across the whole front of the vanguard of Prince Charles's cavalry, commanded by Lord Kilmarnock, which suddenly drew up on the evening of December 21, 1745, to encamp for the night before the Laird of Galabank's house, and he conveyed them by the bridge to Limekilns, a distance of some miles, not being stopped, rather to his surprise. "I did in thoughtless youth," he writes, "what perhaps with some de-
sign would have failed. I saved the horses, and returned in the morning, and saw the clans march through Annandale to Dumfries. Prince Charles walked at the head of the clan Macpherson, which defeated the Duke of Cumberland's horse in a skirmish, and gave some check to the advance of the troops. He was a tall, well made young man; his deportment affable and prince-

Comlongan

ly. When the army crossed the Esk the river was flooded, and the Highlanders had to ford it, nearly 100 packed together to avoid being carried away by the stream. Prince Charles took one of them on his own horse, and desired the officers to do the same." The Highlanders danced a reel to dry themselves.

Limekilns was owned by a staunch adherent of the house of Hanover—Carlile of Bridekirk. While the Prince's army was encamped close to Annan some of his Highlanders went to carouse in the Queensberry Arms, the only inn in the place, and heard Mr Carlile express his opinion very freely on the respective merits of King George and of their young leader. They arrested him, and took him a prisoner to Glasgow. He asked for an interview with the Prince, and told him all that had happened, when the unfortunate Charles replied—"Sir, I commend you for it, and if some of my pretended followers had been so firm in my cause as you are to George, I now should have been on the throne of my fathers." Having said this the Prince let him go. The incident reached the ears of the Duke of Cumberland, who was on his road to the north to attack the Prince's army, and he at once sent for Mr Carlile and offered to relieve him of the heavy debt on his estate if he would assist him with all the information he could; but to the great distress of Mr Carlile's nearest relations, he refused even to meet the Duke. His estate passed out of the hands of his family owing to the general ruin caused by the failure of the local banks after the insurrection was suppressed.

In 1751 James Johnstone, an M.D. of Edinburgh at the age of twenty-one, settled in Worcestershire, for as a younger son he had little hope of inheriting the family estate. After meeting Prince Charles in his youth he was presented with his sons to George III. in his mature age, when his Majesty and Queen Charlotte came to Worcester for the triennial musical festival in 1788. The letters from Scotland to the young physician give a pleasant picture of his paternal home. Although devoted to his profession he found time to return there, and to superintend replanting the Galabank estate. A neighbour, who had been to Worcester, writes from Annan—"I saw old Galabank standing like Boaz among his reapers, and Mrs Johnstone and Mrs Murray came out to speak to me. They particularly asked after little master James." This "little James" was at his grandfather's in 1769 while a dispute was going on about enclosing a common, which in 1771 led to the case of "The Magistrates of the Burgh of Annan against the Marquis of Annandale, Carruthers of Holmains, Johnstone of Galabank," &c. In his letters home he mentions Irving the Apothecary, who was the grandfather of the celebrated preacher Edward Irving, and a tenant of Galabank, and Clapperton, a surgeon in Annan, the father of the traveller Hugh, who was born there in 1788.

The Laird's fifth daughter, Isabella, married John Adam Murray of Belridding, but was early left a widow and returned to her father's house, where her daughter married James Lockhart of Lee and Carnwath, a Lieutenant-General in the Austrian army and a Count of the Holy Roman Empire. Count Lockhart was afterwards made Viceroy of the Netherlands (then an Austrian province). [He left Scotland, having joined Prince Charles, in 1745.] In the memoirs of Madame D'Oberkirch, an ex-governess of the grand Duchess, afterwards Empress of Russia, she describes a visit she paid in 1782, with her old pupil, accompanied by the grand Duke, afterwards the Emperor Paul, to Utrecht, where they were entertained by Lady Lockhart. The Lockharts, she adds, "are an ancient Scotch family, of whom one member was the Ambassador from Cromwell to the Court of France. The Grand Duke, who is very well informed, did not fail to make a delicate allusion to this personage."

Count Lockhart served in the last war which Austria ever waged against the Turks. He was a Knight of the Order of Maria Theresa, and a Lord of the Bedchamber to the Emperor Joseph II.; but on the death of a brother, he inherited the family estates in Scotland. Mrs Lockhart was presented at the Court of Vienna by her cousin, Lord Stormont, the British Ambassador, and the Emperor Joseph II. stood in person as sponsor at the baptism of her eldest son.

Charles Count Wishart Lockhart inherited his father's title, and died in 1802. Sir Simon Lockhart is the present male representative of the family. General Lockhart's daughter, Maryanne Matilda, was, married to Anthony Aufrere, Esq., of Hoveton, Co. York. In the autobiography of James Johnstone (1730-1802) he writes of this niece, "I learn that she gave birth to a daughter, November 17, 1762, at Heidelberg, and that the child was named Louisa Anna Matilda, after Louisa a Princess of Prussia, who with Mrs Aufrere, her mother-in-law, are to be godmothers."

Adam Johnstone, the Laird of Galabank's fifth son, was born February 27, 1732, and received a commission in the Scotch Brigade, which embarked at Aberdeen for Hanover, during the seven years war carried on between the Empress Maria Theresa, and Frederick the Great. The British contingent was placed under the command of the hereditary Prince of Brunswick, in an unsuccessful battle near Wesel, October, 1760, where Adam Johnstone received wounds which caused his death a few days afterwards. The youngest son, Richard, was a Writer to the Signet, and died in London at the age of 28.

The bills for old Galabank's funeral in 1774 are curious as showing the difference in prices at the present time. Painting an escutcheon to put over the house door cost one pound ten shillings, and the frame four shillings and sixpence. The funeral luncheon, which was held at the Queensberry Arms, the only hotel in Annan, consisted of a leg of roast mutton, a pigeon pie, fish and flounders, veal cutlets, chicken, ham, and tarts, for sixteen gentlemen and four ladies, and cost one guinea, exclusive of wine; ten tenants dined in another room for five shillings, and the porter they all drank also cost five shillings. His son James inherited his estate, but continued to live in Worcester. He was the author of nineteen medical works and a classical book, "Dialogues of the Dead," published when a very young man, besides his autobiography and several letters and essays. He is mentioned in "Johnson's Lives of the Poets" as the writer of "a very affecting and instructing account" of the last illness of George Lord Lyttleton, the friend of Pope and Thomson, and according to the second Lord Lyttleton he was both his father's physician and confessor. His eldest son, James, practised as a physician in Worcester, having graduated at the Edinburgh University, where he was a frequent guest at Dryden, General Lockhart's house; and later, when his cousin and her husband returned to Austria, his second brother, Edward, passed a month with them at the viceregal residence. In Howard's "State of English Prisons," he writes of the death of young James Johnstone, who had volunteered gratuitously to attend some prisoners in Worcester gaol when an outbreak of fever had caused a panic through the city. "In the course of my pursuits I have known several amiable young gentlemen who, in their zeal to do good, have been carried off by that dreadful disorder, the gaol fever, and this has been one incentive to my endeavours for its extirpation out of our prisons. I shall mention one affecting instance which happened here (Worcester) of a young physician falling a sacrifice to this distemper through a benevolent attention to some prisoners afflicted with it—Dr Johnstone, junior, of Worcester (1783). He attained at an early period to great and deserved eminence in his profession, and will be ever regretted as a physician of great ability and genius, and as one of the most pleasing and benevolent of men, prematurely snatched from his friends and country."

The Galabank and Westerhall families were then, as they had been earlier, on very friendly terms. Sir William Pulteney, the brother of Sir James Johnstone of Westerhall, presented Dr Johnstone's second son, Thomas, Rector of Fisherton Anger, to the livings of Aston Botterill, Salop, and Hope Bagot, Wilts, in the days when pluralism was allowed, and Dr Johnstone, as ardent a politician as himself, gave him much aid in electioneering. George Johnstone, Sir William's younger brother, and the father of Sir John Lowther Johnstone, was for some years Governor of Florida, and died at Bristol, May 24, 1787. His sister-in-law, writing to inform Dr Johnstone of the event, speaks of him as "my brother and your relation, Governor Johnstone."

Although Dr Johnstone had hoped to end his days in Annandale, where the death of three brothers (the last in 1792) gave him possession of Galabank, the cares of a very large family and of orphan grandchildren kept him in England till his death in 1802, aged 72. A marble tablet to his memory, with a Latin inscription composed by the Rev. Dr Parr, in Worcester Cathedral, is placed under a similar monument to his eldest son. His grandson and heir, James, only survived him three years, so that his third son, Edward, born in 1757, became the head of his house; but owing to a family dispute he bequeathed his Scottish property to his sixth son, John, whose name appears in biographical dictionaries as the author of the "Life of Dr Samuel Parr, D.D." Hence the Scottish estate of Galabank, the last remnant left to them of the barony of Annandale, of which it had once formed a part, has passed into a female branch; and on succeeding his father (1851), Dr Edward Johnstone of Edgbaston Hall, who had lived to the age of 94, the late Mr Edward Johnstone inherited some English property in Worcestershire and Warwickshire, but not the lands of his Scottish ancestors, which they owned in the 15th century. He was a fellow commoner and MA. of Trin. Coll., and a member of the Oxford and Cambridge Club, Pall Mall, having for many years also belonged to the Reform, and been called to the Bar in 1833, but never practised. In 1830-1 the result of the Polish Revolution brought many exiles to this country, and led to the formation of the Literary Association of the Friends of Poland, under the presidency of the poet Campbell, which was joined by the late Lord Dudley Stuart, the late Lord Ilchester, Mr Edward Johnstone, and others, who charitably devoted time and means to alleviate the condition of the refugees. Mr Johnstone—an intimate friend of the late Prince Adam Czartoriski—took the warmest interest in their welfare, and Major Sczulchewski was sent to represent the Society at his funeral in Worcester, September 23, 1881. He was never married, and his eldest nephew, Colonel Sir James Johnstone, K.C.S.I., inherited his estates at Dunsley Manor and Fulford Hall.

The Annandale crest, the spur and wings, is carved on the face of the Queen's College, Birmingham, in memory of the great interest which Dr Edward Johnstone of Edgbaston Hall, [Dr Edward Johnstone married Elizabeth daughter of the late Thomas Pearson, Esq. of Tettenhall, Stafford. She died 1823. He was the first hon. president of the Queen's College, Birmingham, being succeeded by the late Lord Lyttleton.] his younger son James, and his brother John took in its rise and progress from a provincial school of medicine to one of the most important medical colleges in the empire. The same may be said, though their crest does not denote it, of King Edward's School, the General Hospital, and, other benevolent institutions in that literary and scientific town. There, close to the site of the foundation-stone of the Courts of Law laid by Queen Victoria in the year of her jubilee, and in what was then the Old Square, James Johnstone, M.D. of Trin. Coll., F.R.C.P. (born at Edgbaston Hall, 1806; died at Leamington, 1869), long resided, and took a prominent part in the promotion of education in all its branches and other public works within the Midland Metropolis. Besides essays and pamphlets, he published two works on sensation and materia medica. He married Maria Mary Payne, daughter of J. Webster, J.P., of Penns, Co. Warwick, and by her (who died in 1859) he left five sons and seven daughters. The surviving sons are—Colonel Sir James Johnstone, [Late Political Agent at Manipur. He received special commendation in 1879 for his prompt relief on his own responsibility of the headquarters station at Kohima, where nearly 500 British subjects, including English ladies and children, were reduced to the last extremity for want of water, it having been surrounded for a fortnight by 6000 Naga savages. He performed a somewhat similar feat during the Burmese war in 1885-6 to rescue three Englishmen and 250 British native subjects isolated on the Chindwin river; and he was severely wounded in the same campaign.] K.C.S.I., born 1841; married Emma Mary, daughter of S. Lloyd, Esq., late M.P. for Plymouth, and has issue. She died in 1883—Edward settled in Canada— Charles, Captain R.N., of Graitney, Surrey, commanded H.M.S. Dryad at Madagascar, 1883; married Janet, daughter of the late G. Schonswar, Esq., J.P., D.L., formerly M.P. for Hull, and has issue—Richard, in holy orders; married Imogen, daughter of the late W. H. Molesworth, Esq., and has issue. Of the younger sons of Dr James Johnstone of Worcester, fifth laird of Galabank—Henry, fourth son, a colonel in the army, who had seen some service in India and Gibraltar; died at Edgbaston, 1812. John, M.D., F.R.S., died 1836, leaving two daughters. The elder married the late Very Rev. W. F. Hook, Dean of Chichester, and left issue; the younger now owns Galabank. Lockhart, the youngest son, barrister-at-law, Senior Bencher of Gray's Inn, and Commissioner in Bankruptcy, died January, 1861, aged 90, at his house in the Tything, Worcester, leaving John — William, Lieutenant-Colonel, H.E.I.C.S.; died 1887—and two daughters.

James, second Marquis of Annandale, hoping to exclude his half-brothers, made a disposition of his estates in 1726 in favour of his nephew, John Lord Hope, failing whom, to the descendants of his father's sisters, failing whom, to Colonel James Johnstone of Graitney, a cadet of his house. Colonel James Johnstone was Provost of Lochmaben in 1725. He was descended direct from George, the eldest son of William Johnstone of Newbie and Graitney, and it was not then generally known, nor till the recent inquiries into the pedigree necessitated by the claim of the late Mr Edward Johnstone of Fulford Hall to the dormant titles of Annandale, that this George was not born a legitimate son, so that the descendants of John, his younger, but legitimate half-brother, who inherited Newbie, constituted the elder branch. Colonel Johnstone of Graitney assumed the name of Ruthven on his marriage with Isabella, Baroness Ruthven in her own right. She died in 1730, leaving a son James, fourth Baron Ruthven, whose grandson James, sixth Baron, dying without heirs, his sister Mary Elizabeth, whose grandson is the present peer, succeeded to the Ruthven barony.

Chapter Twelve

If the Roman Church in Scotland had been too lax in its discipline and practice, the same fault could not be found with the Presbyterian; [A curious letter exists (1560), signed by Argyll, James Stewart (Regent), and Ruthven, ordering the altars and figures of saints to be turned out of the "Kyrk of Dunkeld," and broken up.] and in Dumfries the Kirk Courts ruled with a severity and interference in domestic affairs during the 17th and 18th centuries which was hardly exceeded by the Inquisition in Italy and Spain. In 1659 nine old women were burned together for witchcraft, and even so late as 1709 a woman was consigned to the flames for the same alleged crime. Slander, Sabbath-breaking, swearing, drinking, and tale-bearing were punished by fines, whipping, the pillory, and sometimes very eccentric penances. A Roman priest, in 1626, was recognised crossing the bridge at Dumfries. He was stopped, but favoured by sympathisers in the crowd contrived to make his escape, while the vestments, altar books, and sacred vessels which he had with him in a bag were seized and burned at the Market Cross. The same was done with the property of another priest in 1658. It was forbidden to send a boy out of the country to be educated in a foreign school; and in 1631 the Privy Council even ordered the son of Lord Nithsdale to be taken from him and educated as a Protestant. In 1628 Herbert Maxwell of Kirkconnel; Gilbert Brown, formerly Abbot of Sweet Heart or Newabbey; his brother Charles; John Williamson in

Lochmaben, and other influential people were ordered to be tried for "Papistry." Sir William Grierson of Lag and Sir John Charteris of Amisfield succeeded in arresting the ex-Abbot and his brother, whereupon their adherents subjected the Protestant minister of Newabbey and his family to ill-usage. In 1647 Lord Herries outwardly conformed to Presbyterianism.

The Scottish Lyon Office, with its contents, having been burned in the last century, and the law being strict in prohibiting the use of armorial bearings unless properly registered, most of the Scottish families matriculated their arms again. The Johnstones of Galabank registered theirs in 1772, and were recorded as belonging to "the family of Newby, an ancient cadet of the Johnstones of Johnstone." Although the tombs of their family of the date of 1649, 1692, and 1726 bore the arms of Johnstone of that Ilk without a difference, the arms of Johnstone of Galabank were registered with a wavy saltire as a mark of cadency, the last Marquis of Annandale being still living; but the late Mr Edward Johnstone, wishing to restore them to the style borne by his direct ancestors, re-matriculated in 1870. The last Marquis died in 1792, when his estates passed to his niece, married to Sir William Hope, who took the name of Johnstone, and their descendant, Mr Hope-Johnstone (born 1842), now owns the ancient barony of Annandale. His brother, Percy Alexander, late Captain 60th Rifles, born 1845, is his heir. He married his cousin, Evelyn Anne, and has issue.

In Sir William Pulteney, the Westerhall family produced one of the most eminent lawyers of the last century, and a distinguished member of the House of Commons. He married the heiress of William Pulteney, Earl of Bath, and took her name. As he left only a daughter, Henrietta Laura, created Countess of Bath in 1792, his baronetcy of Westerhall devolved in 1803 on his nephew, Sir John Lowther Johnstone, the grandfather of the present baronet. The heir to Sir Frederick John William Johnstone is his twin brother, Colonel George Keppel Johnstone, born in 1841. He married Agnes, daughter of Mr Thomas Chamberlayne, and has issue.

There was no minister at Annan or Graitney till about 1612, when Mr Symon Johnstone was appointed to Annan, and remained there many years. Charles I. made enemies of the Scottish landowners in Dumfriesshire as in other parts of Scotland by depriving them of a portion of their tithes, which they exacted from their tenants with far greater severity than had been exercised by the old abbots, to whom their lands had in many instances belonged; and although, when they received these lands, it had been with the stipulation that they should maintain the Parish Kirks this was often done very inadequately. The Johnstones and the Irvings of Bonshaw and Robgill supported Charles, while those noblemen whom his predecessors had enriched with church lands generally supported the Covenanters, particularly the Earl of Buccleuch; for Charles had reversed the attainder of Stewart, Earl of Bothwell, which compelled Buccleuch to restore some of the forfeited lands he had received from James I. The barbarity of the Covenanters in killing the wounded and executing their prisoners is a matter of history, and their subsequent triumph ensured the predominance of Presbyterianism.

In 1706 the representative of the Douglases, the Duke of Queensberry, was the largest proprietor in Dumfriesshire. His title and estates have now passed into a female branch represented by the Duke of Buccleuch, but his nearest male collaterals, the Douglases of Kelhead, succeeded to the titles of Marquis of Queensberry and Viscount Torthorell. The present owner of them has lately sold all his estates in Annandale.

Members for Dumfriesshire and the Burghs of Dumfries, Lochmaben, Annan, and Sanquhar.

An Act of 1427 ordained that "the small barons and free tenants need not come to Parliament nor general counsels, so that of each sheriffdom there be two or three wise men chosen at the head court of the sheriffdom, according to its size." In 1537 another Act ordered the barons to choose one or two of the wisest and most qualified to be Commissioners for the whole shire. In 1587 representation was limited to those who held "a forty shilling land in free tenantry of the King." The Parliaments sat at Scone, Perth, Stirling, or Edinburgh, and the Members voted as one Chamber, there being no division into an Upper and Lower House.

Thos. Lang 1357.
Thos. Welch 1452.
Robert MacBriar 1469.
Nicolas MacBriar 1504.
Herbert Rany 1572.
Patrick MacBriar 1579.
Archibald MacBriar 1581. *(The same year a Dumfriesshire man, John Johnstone, merchant in Edinburgh, sat for that city. He was fourth son of John, Laird of Newbie; married Janet Hunter; died in 1601, leaving a son, John, who settled at Bordeaux, and a daughter, Helen, married to Hugh Dunbar, Writer to the Signet.)*
Robert Cunniughame 1583.
John Maxwell 1585.
Sir Thomas Kirkpatrick 1593. *(He was knighted and made a gentleman of the Privy Chamber by James VI. He fought on the side of Lord Maxwell at the battle of Dryfe Sands, and married Barbara Stewart, daughter of Sir Alexander Stewart of Garlies, .1614.)*
Robert Johnstone, Brigholme and Newbie, Provost of Annan (brother to the M.P. for Edinburgh) 1598.
Sir J. Boswell of Auchinleck 1599.
Herbert Cunningham 1600-1612.
James Cunningham 1605.
William Maxwell 1612.

David Millar 1612.

Francis Irving 1617-25. *(A monument exists to him in Annan churchyard.)*

Sir William Douglas of Drumlanrig, Steward of Annandale 1617.

Sir Wm. Grierson of Lag 1617-25.

John Corsell 1617.

Edward Johnstone of Ryehill and Newbie 1627-28-33.

Sir John Charteris—1621-25, 28-33.

Nicoll Cunningham 1621.

John Crichton of Rayhill 1628-33.

Robert MacBriar, Laird of Almagill— 1630-46-47-48.

William Fergusson 1640-41.

Thomas Kirkpatrick of Closeburn 1639-41. *(In case of absence Sir John Charteris of Amisfield, his father-in-law.)*

Sir John Charteris 1639-41. *(He married a daughter of William Crichton, Earl of Dumfries.)*

John Corsane 1621-28-33.

John Johnstone of MyInfield and Galabank 1640-42, 1644-47.

Homer Murray -1643.

John Irving 1630-39-41.

George Johnstone of Galabank 1644-46-47.

Lawrence Davidson 1643-49.

Cuthbert Cunninghame, Advocate 1643.

John Kennedy 1643.

John Laurie 1643.

John Henderson 1645-47-48-61-63.

William Douglas 1644-48-49.

Sir Alexander Jardine 1645-46.

Robert Fergusson of Craigdarroch 1649-50-51, 61-63-65-67-69-72-78.

John Fergusson. 1649.

William Crichton 1645-47.

Sir James Douglas 1644-49-50-51.

Sir William Douglas *(created Earl of Queensberry)* 1647.

Sir James Johnstone *(created Earl of Annandale, &c.)* 1654-56.

Jeremy Tolhurst 1654-55, 59-60.

James Douglas of Mouswald 1649-50-51.

James Crichton, Sheriff of Dumfries 1661-63.

John Williamson 1661-63.

Robert Carmichael, Provost of Sanquhar 1665-67-69-72-78 81-82.

William Graham of Blaatwood 1609-72.

James Carruthers, Provost of Annan 1681-82.

John Irving 1661-65-67-69-74.

Hugh Sinclair of Inglistoune 1661-3, 1665-7.

David Johnstone of Galabank, Bailie of Annan 1678.

Sir Robert Dalziell 1667-69-74-81-82-85-86.

William Craig, Provost of Dumfries 1678-81-82.

Sir John Dalziell 1686-89-90.
Sir Thos. Kirkpatrick 1690-1702.
Thomas Kennedy 1685-86-89 to 1695.
John Boswell 1689-92.
Sir James Johnstone of Westerhall 1689-1700.
James Johnstone of Corehead 1690-93.
John Johnstone of Elsiechellis, Bailie of Lochmaben 1665 67-69-74-81-82. *(Provost.)*
John Sharp of Collistoun 1686.
Robert Johnstone 1695-1702-7.
William Crichton 1690 till 1702.
Alexander Johnstone of Elsiechellis 1693-1702.
Alex. Bruce 1692-1702 *(expelled).*
William Alves 1702-7.
Sir William Johnstone of Westerhall 1698 to 1722.
Alexander Fergusson 1702-7.
James Lord Johnstone 1708.
Sir John Johnstone of Westerhall 1700-8.
William Paterson, founder of the Bank of England and projector of the Darien Scheme 1708.
Mr Sharp of Hoddam 1702-7.
Sir Wm. Grierson 1709-11.
Dr John Hutton, M.D., of Padua—1710-13. *(He accompanied William III. at the battle of the Boyne.)*
Alexander Fergusson 1715-22.
William Douglas of Cavers 1722.27.
Charles Erskine of Barjarg 1722-41.
Hon. James Murray 1711-13.
Sir J. Douglas 1735-47.
Wm. Kirkpatrick 1736-8.
Sir Robert Laurie 1738-41
Lord John Johnstone *(elected under age)* 1741. *(Died in 1743.)*
Sir James Johnstone of Westethall, Provost of Lochmaben 1743-54.
James Veitch 1755-60.
Charles Douglas, Earl of Drumlanrig 1747-54.
William Douglas of Kelhead 1768-80.
Thomas Miller, Lord Advocate 1761-66.
James Montgomery 1766-68.
General Archibald Douglas of Kirkton 1754-61-68-74.
Sir R. Herries—1780-84.
Sir James Johnstone of Westerhall 1784-90.
Capt. Patrick Miller 1790-6.

County.

General Sir R. Laurie 1774-1804.
Vice-Admiral Sir Wm. J. Hope 1804-30.
Viscount Drumlanrig *(late Marquis of Queensberry)* 1847-57.
John H. Hope-Johnstone of Raehills 1830-47, 57-65.
Colonel Walker of Crawfordton 1865-68, 69-74.
Sir S. Waterlow 1868.
John J. Hope-Johnstone 1874-80.
Sir Robert Jardine of Castlemilk 1880, et seq.

Burghs.

Hon. A. Hope 1796-1834.
Vice-Admiral Sir Wm. Johnstone Hope 1800-2.
Right Hon. Charles Hope 1802-3.
Viscount Stopford 1803-6.
Sir J. Heron Maxwell 1807.
Lord Wm. Robt. K. Douglas 1812-32.
General Matthew Sharpe of Hoddam 1833-41.
Win. Ewart 1847-68.
Sir Robert Jardine of Castlemilk 1868-74.
Ernest Noel 1874-86.
R. T. Reid, Q.C. 1886.

Provosts of Dumfries Down to 1700.

Robert. Macbriar 1469.	Matthew Dickson 1582.
T. Welsh 1471.	John Marshal 1583.
Robert Macbriar 1472.	Simon Johnstone 1584.
Robert Macbriar 1549.	Alexander Maxwell 1585.
John Macbriar 1552.	Herbert Rayning 1586.
Archibald Macbriar 1570.	John Bryce 1587.
Herbert Rayning 1572.	Roger Gordon 1588.
Archibald Macbriar 1575.	Herbert Rayning 1591-2.
Robert Macbriar 1578.	Homer Maxwell 1593.
Robert Macbriar 1579.	Lord Maxwell 1596.
Archibald Macbriar 1581.	

In 1607 the Lords of the Privy Council directed the town replace Maxwell, then outlawed for the murder of Johnstone, by Sir R. Kirkpatrick.

Herbert Cunningham—1612.	John Corsane—1642.
Doubtful.	Robert Grahame—1643.
John Corsane—1622.	John Maxwell—1645.
Sir Roger Kirkpatrick—1623.	Thomas Macburnie—1649 to 1654.
John Corrie—1639.	John Irving—1660 to 1665.

Thomas Irving—1665 to 1668.
John Irving—1668 to 1674.
Lord Drumlanrig—1683 to 1686.
John Maxwell—1687 to 1688.

Thomas Rome—1691.
Robert Johnstone and John Irving,
alternately, till 1700.

In 1517 the Bailies of Dumfries were:—John Welsh, Andro Airying, John Ranyng, Adam Edzair, Edward of Johnstone, David Wilson, Thomas Macnaughton, George Curror, Herbert Gladstanes, Adam Wallace, James Kirkpatrick, David Cunningham.

In 1543—Edward Johnstone, John Crosbie, George Maxwell, Thomas Maxwell, Herbert Gladstanes, Herbert Parsons, Herbert Maxwell, Gilbert Macbyrnie, Andro Airying, William Paterson, Homer Maxwell, Anthony Houston, Robert Crawfurd, Thomas Ranyng.

In 1575—Herbert Baillie, William Gladstanes, Thomas Johnstone, Thos. Baty, William Paterson, Andro Moresone, Herbert Maxwell, Peter Davidson, James Wallace, Michael Newall, John Hereis, Andro Edzar, Herbert Ranyng, David Rae, John Roule.

On the accession of George I., and far into the reign of George III., this oath was required from the Provosts and Bailies, or any holding public office, in Dumfriesshire:—

"I, the underscribed, do truly and sincerely acknowledge, and declare in my conscience before God and the World, that my Sovereign, King George, is lawful and rightful King of Great Britain, and all other his Majesty's dominions thereunto belonging, and I do solemnly and sincerely declare that I do believe in my conscience that the person pretended to be Prince of Wales during the life of the late King James, and since his decease pretending to be or taking upon himself the style and title of King of England by the name of James III., or of Scotland by the name of James VIII., or the style and title of King of Great Britain, had not any right or title whatsoever to the Crown of this realm, or any other dominion thereunto belonging. . . . and I will do my utmost to disclose and make known to his Majesty and his successors all treason and traitorous attempts which I shall know to be against him," &c. "So help me God."

In 1714, Abraham Crichton was Provost of Sanquhar, and John Crichton (two), Robert Fisher, William Macwath, James Stewart, &c., Bailies. At Sanquhar the Crichton family had almost the monopoly of the Provostship.

Stewards Depute of Annandale—1609, John Johnstone in Mylnfield; 1610, John Carruthers of Holmains; 1611, Master John Johnstone; 1613, John Carruthers.

The register of births, deaths, and marriages in Dumfries is not older than 1620, and is very much broken till the end of that century. Some of the entries are curious. Boys are registered as man bairns, and girls as maid bairns; and there is often a description of the person whose death is recorded, such as "a poor old woman," "a lame begging man," &c.; and in one instance the incumbent details the ancestry and virtues of his mother-in-law. The records of the burgh are preserved with intervals from 1479. The register of Dumfriesshire sasines, which begins in 1618, are lost during the years of Civil War, as is also the Register of Wills, and almost every other record relating to Dumfriesshire at that period.

Ancient Provosts of Annan

Lord Maxwell—1591.
Robert Johustone of Brigholme and Newbie—1598.
John Johnstone of Newbie *(nephew to the above)*—1602.
Master of Maxwell—1606. *(The Lords in Council directed the town to replace him by Sir William Cranstoun in 1607, on account of the murder of the Lord of Johnstone by Lord Maxwell.)*
Edward Johnstone of Ryehill and Newbie—1612.
Robert Johnstone of Broomhills—1617.
Robert Johnstone of Raecleuch *(tutor and nearest heir to the Laird of Johnstone)*—1618.
Edward Johnstone of Ryehill—1619.
David Millar—1621.
Abraham Johnstone of Brume and Newbie, brother to Edward— 1622. *(Specimens of their handwriting exist in connection with their office.)*
David Millar—1625.
John Johnstone of Mylnfield—1624, and from 1638 to 1643.
Homer Murray (of the Cockpool family)—1643.
George Johnstone of Mylnfield; also Parliamentary Commissioner— 1646.
John Johnstone of Mylnfield—1649.
Mark Loch—1656. *(He was the first lessee of the Government Post between Carlisle and Annan.)*
Hugh Sinclair— 1661.
Bryce Blair—1666.
William Grahame of Blaatwood—1669 and 1683. *(He married a Carlile of Bridekirk.)*
William Johnstone, Earl of Annandale—1670.
David Johnstone, brother to John of Mylnfield *(then dead)*—1678.
James Carruthers—1681.
John Johnstone of Galabank—1682.
Bryce Blair—1685.
Earl of Annandale, created Marquis—1686 till 1713.
James Lord Johnstone—1713.
Bryce Blair, John Johnstone of Galabank, J. Irving, and others in the last century.

Appendices

Appendix A - Sovereigns of Scotland.

Kenneth II.
Duncan I.— 1034.
Macbeth—1040.
Malcolm III.—1056.
Donald —1093.
Duncan II.—1094.
Edgar—1097.
Alexander I.—1106.
David I.—1124.
Malcolm IV.—1153.
William the Lyon—1165.
Alexander II.—1214.
Alexander III. —1249.
Margaret—1286.
John Baliol—1292.
Sir William Wallace, Guardian
Robert Bruce—1306.
David II.—1329.
Robert II—1370.
Robert III.---1390.---Illegitimate.

Duke of Albany, Regent—1405.
James I—1423.
James II.—1437.
James III.—1460.
James IV.—1488.
James V. —1513.
Mary—1542.
James VI.—1567.
Charles I.—1625.
Cromwell—1649.
James VII.—1685.
Charles II.—1660.
William III. and Mary II.—1688.
Anne—1702.
George I—1714.
George II.—1727.
George III.—1760.
George IV.—1820.
William IV.---1830.
Victoria—1837.

Appendix B - Royal Descent of the Bruces

Royal Descent of the Bruces ; Carlyles of Torthorwald, Bridekirk, and Limekilns ; Johnstones of Galabank and Fulford Hall ; Corries ; Stewarts, &c.

As Daughters of Scottish Kings generally married Scotsmen, a large number of Scottish Noblemen claim Royal descent.

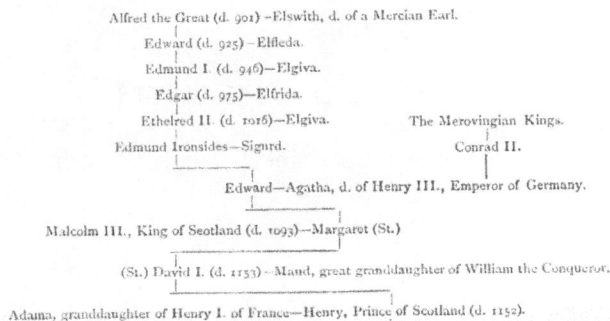

Alfred the Great (d. 901) –Elswith, d. of a Mercian Earl.

Edward (d. 925) – Elfleda.

Edmund I. (d. 946)—Elgiva.

Edgar (d. 975)—Elfrida.

Ethelred II. (d. 1016)—Elgiva.   The Merovingian Kings.

Edmund Ironsides—Sigurd.   Conrad II.

Edward—Agatha, d. of Henry III., Emperor of Germany.

Malcolm III., King of Scotland (d. 1093)—Margaret (St.)

(St.) David I. (d. 1153) – Maud, great granddaughter of William the Conqueror.

Adama, granddaughter of Henry I. of France—Henry, Prince of Scotland (d. 1152).

116

William, King of Scotland (d. 1214). David (d. 1219), m. Maud, d. of Earl of Chester,

Alexander II. Robert Bruce—Isabel (illegitimate).

(2) Robert Bruce—Isabel. (1) Margaret (Baliol's line). Walter, High Steward.

Robert (d. 1295)—Isabel de Clare. Earl of Carrick—Marjory.

Robert (d. 1303)—Margaret, Countess of Carrick.

King Robert I. Margaret—Sir W. Carlile descended rom Malcolm II.

Walter, High Steward—Marjory.

(2) Thomas (d. 1346). (3) John. Wm. de Carlyle (described as sister's son to the King).

Robert de Corry—Susanna. William.

Left issue. Sir John Carlyle (d. 1400).

Sir John (d. before 1435)—m. Elizabeth Kirkpatrick.

Sir William (d. before 1468). Robert, Governor of Thrieve Castle.

Margaret. m. Sir Wm. Douglas of Drumlanrig, ancestor to Marquis of Queensberry. Sir John, 1st Lord Carlile. Adam of Bridekirk, ancestor of the Carliles of Ponsbourne Park, Herts, and Gayhurst, Bucks; of Col. Thos. Bell; and of the Johnstones of Galabank and Fulford Hall. James, Rector of Kirkpatrick.

Appendix C - Letters from Carlyle, The Historian, and Edward Irving

Craigenputtock, 18th July, 1829.

MY DEAR IRVING,— I write in very great haste, and to write a favor must therefore proceed directly to business. Mr Andrew Anderson, the youngest and now only British son (for the other two are in India) of the Straquhan family, is setting out for Birmingham to establish himself there as surgeon. He reckons that it would essentially serve him to be introduced to Dr (John) Johnstone of Galabank, the chief physician there. He has already seen Dr J., and been kindly received by him, but only under the escort of some transient and merely official acquaintance, and only in the character of an aspirant to medical employment without further testimonial of any kind. I believe you knew Mr Anderson's brother. . . . Could you now, on the faith of my evidence, testify to Dr Johnstone that our young adventurer is a person of the same stamp. An honest, inoffensive, diligent, even amiable and praiseworthy man, would be much assisted thereby, an old friend gratified, and a worthy and much afflicted family cheered and obliged. As your whole knowledge must be by hearsay, I am careful not to exaggerate Mr A.'s praises. What I have stated may be repeated as mine in all situations without fear of contradiction. A letter of this purport to Dr Johnstone, and sent under cover to "A. Anderson, Esq., 68 High Street, Birmingham," would accomplish all that is wanted. . . I have made no engagement for your performing the kindness, ex-

117

cept the assurance that you were at all times a warm-hearted, helpful man, and delighted in nothing so much as in assisting all that needed assistance. Had you seen the young man himself, or seen his mother (one of the most estimable Scottish ladies and mothers I have ever seen, and now widowed and sick, yet trusting meekly in a higher guidance), you would rejoice to do this much for her sake, and far more.

And, now, I must leave the matter in your own hands, for, as hinted above, I have not a minute to myself. I am scribbling against time, and sore held back by many things, chiefly by natural dulness.

We feel glad that we saw you here. Your presence, as it always does, has brightened up our regard for you, and dissipated all newspaper tarnish, if there ever was such. Even your errors of opinion (as I must consider them) assume a respectable shape, errors of a good heart, and a strong, though too luxuriant, intellect. We take you as you are, and are very glad that we have you.

The bruit of your appearance is not yet dead in this quarter, and the old grey crag still stands (where it has stood since the deluge).

Thomas Carlyle.

To the Rev. Edward Irving.

London, 13 Judd Place, East,
21st December, 1829.

MY DEAR AND HONOURED FRIEND,— If I be not troublesome, I desire to introduce to you my young friend, Dr John Carlyle, an Annandale man, the brother of the very ingenious man at whose request I introduced Mr Anderson to you some time ago. Dr Carlyle is a young man of excellent character and principles, great modesty, honesty, and simplicity, well bred, and well learned in his profession, so far as I am a judge. He has resided on the Continent, and in Germany, for some years in the house of one of the chief men of the Bavarian Court as his friend; but he has brought home with him the same Scottish character for morals and principles with which he went out. He intends practising at Warwick as a physician, and I err greatly if he will not prove a credit to a profession which your father's name has already raised to such a height in these parts. I commend him to your kindness, and to that of my dear and most kind friend, Mrs Johnstone. My respectful love to all your house, and to your brother; and to your daughter and her husband, when you see them.

Your affectionate and faithful friend,

Edward Irving.
To Dr John Johnstone,
Monument House.